Storytelling

The Ultimate Playbook to Master the Art

(How to Increase Your Impact, Influence and Income With the Power of Stories)

Matthew Burgess

Published By **Andrew Zen**

Matthew Burgess

All Rights Reserved

Storytelling: The Ultimate Playbook to Master the Art (How to Increase Your Impact, Influence and Income With the Power of Stories)

ISBN 978-0-9938301-5-0

No part of this guidebook shall be reproduced in any form without permission in writing from the publisher except in the case of brief quotations embodied in critical articles or reviews.

Legal & Disclaimer

The information contained in this book is not designed to replace or take the place of any form of medicine or professional medical advice. The information in this book has been provided for educational & entertainment purposes only.

The information contained in this book has been compiled from sources deemed reliable, and it is accurate to the best of the Author's knowledge; however, the Author cannot guarantee its accuracy and validity and cannot be held liable for any errors or omissions. Changes are periodically made to this book. You must consult your doctor or get professional medical advice before using any of the suggested remedies, techniques, or information in this book.

Upon using the information contained in this book, you agree to hold harmless the Author from and against any damages, costs, and expenses, including any legal fees potentially resulting from the application of any of the information provided by this guide. This disclaimer applies to any damages or injury caused by the use and application, whether directly or indirectly, of any advice or information presented, whether for breach of contract, tort, negligence, personal injury, criminal intent, or under any other cause of action.

You agree to accept all risks of using the information presented inside this book. You need to consult a professional medical practitioner in order to ensure you are both able and healthy enough to participate in this program.

Table Of Contents

Chapter 1: Why Are We Capable To Inform Stories? 1

Chapter 2: The Storyteller's Mindset 8

Chapter 3: Building And Making Prepared Your Story 21

Chapter 4: The Beginning 40

Chapter 5: Warm Up In Advance Than Getting On Degree 51

Chapter 6: Overcoming Fear And Mastering To Like The Level 70

Chapter 7: What Is Powerful Storytelling? 77

Chapter 8: The Descriptive And Referential Segment: 86

Chapter 9: Storytelling And Severa Worldwide 95

Chapter 10: Crafting Of Captive Business Employer Narrative 109

Chapter 11: How To Shake Up Your Storytelling Fashion 122

Chapter 12: The Real Struggle 136

Chapter 13: Create Rapport With Them 152

Chapter 14: The Right Attitude And Power 175

Chapter 1: Why Are We Capable To Inform Stories?

Before we get into the beef of a way to create and supply an evocative tale, we need to first take a look at why recollections are so valuable to us as human beings. Where does the almost hypnotic energy they have over us come from? How and why do they impact us so deeply?

The psychology of Storytelling

Like most of our behaviors, storytelling is rooted deep in our psychology, which in turn is mostly a end give up result of our evolutionary development as a species. Human beings fee patterns — we be aware and charge cause and effect. It's what permits us to make experience of the world spherical us. At its middle, a tale is really that: a educate of motive and impact. The teller recounts an event that brought on each unique, which in flip delivered about each different, and so on until they achieve a end.

This is usually how the actual worldwide works, and we acquired our massive gain over precise species at the same time as we observed to recognize this.

It's due to this that narrative, the manner that topics come together in a logical collection is so essential to us. We see it in the international spherical us, and we massively enjoy discovering it. Stories engage that deep-seated preference for narrative, beautiful it with the useful aid of giving the listener a glimpse into the way it genuinely works within the existence of the character telling the tale.

If you have got were given a message, there are approaches you may pass approximately handing over it. Suppose you want to percentage with an goal market of younger people who need to pursue the same career you have got got. You ought to just supply them a sterile listing of the whole lot they want to do to obtain what you have got – the regions of observe they may must attention on, the quantity of exertions they'll have to installed, the limitations they will face – in a widespread revel in that isn't too tailored to any character. You'd use wording like "most successful actors had to live for years taking low-paying bit components as extras or in commercials" or "in case you want to be a successful realtor, you'll must in detail apprehend how the housing marketplace works".

On the possibility hand, you could deliver your recommendation within the form of a tale – in this situation your tale mainly. An actor ought to inform the story of his private period of lowly paid obscurity, and the realtor may additionally need to offer personal anecdotes of what she studied, how a good buy effort and time it took you and the barriers she confronted. If a few elements of the climb to wherein they'll be now did now not work out to them, they may fill those gaps in with the memories of your colleagues.

On the floor the number one approach looks as if it would artwork thoroughly – the advice could have a look at to everybody, leaving no place for really anybody to anticipate it wouldn't paintings for them mainly. But in reality the second method could in fact be some distance extra powerful. Studies have proven that once a first-rate duration, most effective 5-10% of records this is handed on as easy statistics remains sparkling and colorful within the mind of the character receiving it, however an incredible sixty five-70% of information handed on inside the shape of recollections is retained. Why is that this so?

Well, the motive for that is that smooth records activate regions of the thoughts that decipher which means that...and now not something else. Raw records truely aren't very stimulating in any respect. When paying attention to a tale, however, a few very interesting matters arise inside the mind. Parts of the mind that could be activated if the people listening have been without a doubt doing the matters being defined are activated. If the storyteller is describing a motion, say like taking walks or dancing, the motor cortex, it truly is liable for controlling our movements lighting fixtures up. If the storyteller describes a sensory input, like a scent, a taste or the feeling of a texture, the sensory cortex, which decodes actual sensory inputs, is activated. This is on top of the reactive feelings we experience at the identical time as being attentive to a tale: an define of a disturbing or horrifying state of affairs induces tension and fear with the useful resource of proxy, and the selection of such situations brings palpable comfort. Descriptions of love and glad conditions deliver us that warmness, fuzzy feeling inner as though we are experiencing them ourselves.

As a quit result, a story an extended manner greater without issue and virtually imprints itself within the reminiscences of the listener. The records of the story and the emotions it brings up in this manner act as a transport mechanism in your information or message, sporting it along and helping it 'stick' in the audience's brains. One particular demonstration of the strength of stories to imprint themselves inside the brain of a listener is how they once in a while turn out to be this kind of large part of their psyche that they start to tell the story as even though they have been present or as even though it virtually befell to them. Sure, an entire lot of times this is accomplished for easy effect, or as outright robbery; however an thoughts-blowing variety of instances it's really genuinely unconscious. The tale changed into so nicely knowledgeable, the photos it left so colourful that the listener has absolutely forgotten that it didn't simply take region to them.

The value of a story isn't simply relying on the shape of information it offers to the target market. The emotions and reactions it creates can be immensely treasured clearly via manner of themselves. Implanting feelings in the mind of each other person the manner a story does is a exceedingly effective element, helping their brains to are available in sync with yours. This may be of splendid price whilst you are trying to steer others to count on your way – priming them together collectively with your very own forms of notion and feeling makes them a whole lot greater open to a few exclusive mind you could want for them to undertake. Telling the tale of an occasion or situation that commonplace who you are can affect your goal market the very identical way because of the truth the occasion itself affected you.

On the whole, we are in a role to infer that there are four primary desires one desires to gain while telling a story. In no particular order, they're – to entertain, to tell, to teach and to encourage. All tales aim to reap a few combination of those, and they'll be typically the maximum green and prolonged-lasting manner of doing it.

Chapter 2: The Storyteller's Mindset

Now which you've stuck a small glimpse of methods and why recollections have an impact on us the manner they do, you no question need to apprehend a way to harness and follow that energy successfully. It's tempting to want to leap immediately to the element where you studies what to do on the equal time as you rise up within the spotlight and all the recommendations and tricks for you to get the aim marketplace right away into the palm of your hand, but this will be leaping the gun thru quite a chunk.

The truth is that an tremendous story starts off evolved prolonged before you hit the volume, in fact lengthy earlier than you even realize that there can be going to be a talking engagement that could require you to inform a story. The very first steps begin with you becoming a storyteller, and adopting the mind-set of 1. This financial disaster will check what it is that makes an excellent storyteller, and in so doing assist you for your manner to becoming one.

A lot of humans are hesitant to upward push up on diploma and tell a tale. A big a part of this is fear of the extent itself: being the focal point of attention is absolutely considered considered one of our primal fears, so that is quite understandable. We will have a have a look at how to conquer this worry in a while, but an trouble of maximum human being's aversion to storytelling that is regularly disregarded is that a whole lot of us keep in mind we just don't have any suitable tales to tell that would hobby or decorate different humans, and that not anything they've heard, executed or professional need to ever preserve the attention of an audience.

This is virtually obviously unfaithful. No people's lives are exactly the equal, and every unmarried character has a very precise set of reviews, in addition to a totally precise worldview with which we interpret those reviews. As we've already visible, a part of the cause we inform reminiscences is to percentage in every precise's lives and benefit a gllmpse into how others outside of ourselves anticipate and sense, so even the maximum apparently common and banal testimonies of your existence are capability property of material. Interesting topics take region to and round us all of the time, and the simple fact is that maximum oldsters are ignorant of those gadgets.

The first step to turning into a brilliant storyteller is to triumph over the notion that you do not have something interesting to percentage with others. Once you've got were given certainly embraced the philosophy that your life may be a source of thrilling and inspirational recollections, you may discover that super new vistas organizing themselves to you.

To located the philosophy in exercising, always be observant and present in each interplay that you have. What sets unique storytellers aside from absolutely everyone else – be it the fellow for your circle of buddies who by no means appears to have a lack of testimonies to inform or the the world over acclaimed speaker who often goes inside the front of audiences numbering inside the heaps – is they constantly pass into every interaction they've got and look into the whole lot that takes location in their lives searching out stories. You need to additionally have the identical attitude. If you look for interesting things that appear in your life, you may locate them.

If you observe the advice given later in this e-book, you may have a message or lesson you want to deliver at the identical time as you're telling a story. Such education have a dependency of popping up in locations wherein you least assume them, or of most effective being apparent looking again while you come back to recollect them later in life. An experience may additionally seem absolutely random and beside the point on the time it is taking place to you, but you could never apprehend – it is able to flip out useful to demonstrate a few difficulty you will in no manner have concept it could.

This technique is also relevant to constructing a story of your lifestyles that spans years. A type of times you may be referred to as upon or may also additionally moreover need to tell reminiscences about subjects that passed off over a protracted span of time – recounting your career, the story of methods you wooed your partner or a duration of problem you confronted, to offer some examples. Every such narrative is built up of character occasions, and you can no longer be able to assemble it up and tell it convincingly without the ones seemingly insignificant info. Similar to how instructions that can be extracted from events are sometimes fine obvious looking again, the extra usual tale is pretty regularly invisible to you even as you are in the center of it. Always pay interest to what is round you, regardless of whether or not it appears top notch at the time or not.

Of course, you typically obtained't be the only man or woman in your recollections, and neither will you only need to or be requested to recount recollections about yourself. You may additionally moreover select out or be required to inform a tale approximately every extraordinary character to your life, a tale wherein you could now not moreover be involved. To do this well you may obviously need a deeper than superficial interest in and know-how of the humans spherical you. As nicely as being attentive to the sports in your personal life, assemble an hobby in the subjects that take area inside the lives of others. Be observant while you have interaction with them so that you can get a sense for their personalities and listen to their very personal recollections. This way you will be able to weave well-rounded and correct representations of their characters, similarly to add every other deliver of material into your arsenal.

Another type of story you may be requested to tell are fictional memories – legends, famous memories and myths. Having a previous hobby and data of these will help you a tremendous deal. If you are normally analyzing and listening to one of a kind human beings inform those stories, you may initially have a higher understanding of the way they arrive together and of approaches to inform them, and you may additionally have a number of them prepared to installation whilst you are asked to speak.

Usually, growing your non-public fictitious situations is the realm of the written phrase, but there are instances while doing so may be appropriate, or you're mainly requested to do truly that. Some examples of situations in which that can be suitable encompass speaking approximately an enjoy you have not any direct or 2nd-hand experience of, or if you are tackling a very sensitive state of affairs in which you may want to shield identities or understand the privacy of human beings who've skilled it, or you want to make a factor that you may't pretty hit proper on the top with some aspect you've skilled in actual lifestyles.

All of the guidelines given above also are vitally essential in case you want to install writing brilliant, conceivable and enriching fictional memories. A authentic fictional tale, regardless of how fantastical it's far, has its roots in reality and within the not unusual human stories we percent. Being conscious of the subjects that seem spherical you may offer masses of idea and give you a strong base from which to weave your tale. Your characters can even should be workable so as on your target audience to connect with them, so you will want a extra than number one understanding of techniques other human beings in reality assume and behave. Reading and being attentive to terrific fictional memories will also come up with a sense of strategies they may be constructed and the way first rate to supply them.

Of path, it can be difficult to hold a intellectual tally of all your memories and feature the ability to tug one up at will and in detail, so that you will probable need to record your research in some shape this is a whole lot less fallible than your memory. A actual idea is to keep a magazine in which you write down topics that appear to you each day that are interesting or have some shape of moral or private significance. You don't want to move into minute element – a simple outline of the factors of the revel in that stood out to you the maximum is going to be sufficient to jog your memory while you appearance lower back on it at a later time. From time to time take a look back via your magazine and examine the belongings you wrote in the past. This serves a dual reason – it allows you to view the activities within the mild of hindsight, while their area inside the fundamental narrative of your life is lots clearer, and it moreover refreshes your reminiscence so that you can more without hassle recollect them at the same time as you are making organized your story.

Similarly, you need to furthermore record the testimonies you have got got been recommended by way of using the use of the humans around you of their personal reviews in your magazine, further to extraordinary types of memories that you pay hobby or study so that you can better don't forget them at the identical time as you want to.

On pinnacle of all this, an remarkable storyteller realizes that she or he might be able to by no means have a look at sufficient approximately the craft. No depend how superior you switch out to be as a storyteller, there will continuously be extra room for improvement. There will continuously be extra you could studies, every other approach you can lease if you want to make your memories most effective a bit bit greater attractive and entire.

With this in mind, continuously be looking for possibilities to growth your capabilities. There are lots of books that train a manner to write down down higher tales and the manner to decorate your presence and ability at the degree. Always be looking for books like folks who allow you to end up higher at storytelling. You also can discover instructions that educate on storytelling and public speaking. If you have got a college or university close by, they will commonly have open instructions that you could sign up in, or even in case you don't, you likely no matter the fact that have the best tool for discovering data to be had at your fingertips. The internet is a extremely good resource – you could discover publications and tutorials on many precise internet websites devoted to continuing training, similarly to on streaming web web sites like YouTube.

A actual storyteller also realizes that it is not possible to take a look at in a vacuum. All the schooling and intellectual reinforcement of storytelling beliefs in the global can in no way be enough – you need to have a observe others doing it in addition to gather remarks to your very very own approach.

Watch as many exclusive storytellers doing their trouble, be it live or recorded. Befriend and loaf around unique storytellers and use them to change thoughts and studies from them, especially individuals who are higher at it than you and you aspire to emulate. Not to say that you shouldn't spend time with individuals who are nevertheless developing toward your degree, though – searching them for errors will allow you to pick out out some of your private, and instructing others is one of the outstanding methods of gaining knowledge of.

Storytelling groups and small-scale, close by storytelling occasions are beginning to advantage pretty numerous recognition in most fundamental cities these days. These are an brilliant manner to find like-minded humans and a region to beautify yourself as a storyteller. They are usually more snug and characteristic a superb deal decrease stakes than an event in which you have got a huge target market or a number of pressure to get it right in a unmarried shot. As a stop result, you've got have been given a more supportive environment in which you can try new topics and fail until you get it right without worry of losing a high opportunity to get a component across.

Working on your mindset is a never-completing machine. You will continuously need to preserve watch over your thoughts, making sure you approach each unmarried experience with a view of the way you could flip it into an awesome tale and in no way passing up an possibility to hone your craft, have a study and look at from others. As lengthy as you stay with this you can keep to beautify and come to be a better and better storyteller.

Chapter 3: Building And Making Prepared Your Story

Once you've started out the continual method of refining your thoughts-set, there's however lots more training that desires to be accomplished earlier than you can get your story out on degree. The next series of steps begins offevolved as soon as you've got confirmation of the occasion – you have got were given been invited or common as a speaker, and now apprehend the date, the venue, the make-up of the purpose market, the situation and different specifics. It's at this component that you begin getting ready for the unique occasion, tailoring your tale and making ready your thoughts for it.

This degree of training is essential – it's wherein you sincerely craft and excellent the story itself. Lack of training manifests itself in quite a few bad techniques at the degree – your story can be disjointed, lack emotional effect and fail to supply substantial statistics. It may additionally even manifest itself in you bodily and mentally – not knowing your tale inner and out reasons nervousness and all the tics and issues related to it.

This bankruptcy goes to provide you with a step-through-step manual to developing a tale with a purpose to no longer fine waft like water out of your thoughts but may even flow into the minds of the goal marketplace in a manner so as to have interaction them and go away them enriched and satisfied.

STEP 1: Figure out your purpose

We took a have a take a look at the objectives of storytelling again within the first bankruptcy. Figuring out what your desires might be in telling your story goes to be the first aspect you do whilst making ready for the real night time time of your retelling. Your intention will guide the whole thing else you do from proper here on, from choosing the precise enjoy you can draw from, all of the way through to the way you carry yourself on the volume.

First of all, no matter what unique conditions you could have, you could want to keep your aim market's interest. With this in mind, being interesting isn't always without a doubt an desire but a necessity. Being thrilling doesn't first-class advocate maintaining your target market rollicking with laughter or gasping and shouting with exhilaration, even though. An interesting tale is one which engages the goal marketplace's emotions, and this consists of the entire gamut from entertainment and pleasure to pathos (the feeling of commiserative pity and unhappiness), choice, affection and encouragement. Emotion is what connects us to every one-of-a-type, and this want to be the regular in all the recollections you inform.

The specifics of the event will dictate which of the alternative targets you'll take upon yourself to meet. Sometimes it will likely be sufficient honestly to entertain – this is especially authentic of exceptional and informal environments. If you're swapping testimonies with pals round a campfire or in a bar then through all manners, preserve your story as moderate and fun as viable. Most scheduled occasions wherein you are invited to talk will commonly need something more from you, no matter the reality that. The objective of those is usually no longer certainly to have a remarkable time but to move away the purpose market knowing, having located or gained a few factor they didn't have previously and possibly wouldn't have without taking note of your tale.

STEP 2: Have a message or moral in your tale and be part of it in conjunction with your evaluations

This step is intricately tied in with the preceding one and serves the same aim: giving your tale recognition and your target market some aspect they can put off from the tale, the distinction being that your intention is definitely for you own on my own even as your message can be explicitly stated and is a way for your goal market to connect to your tale.

To make your message stick, you need to tie it in together with your evaluations. You need to draw an immediate connection among them in order that they beautify each specific. There are hints from which you may technique the relationship amongst your message and your tales. Sometimes you'll be given a selected message you are purported to carry, or it'll be dictated via manner of manner of the context of the event – specifically the audience you're talking to. In the ones instances you want to pick out a story from your monetary organization that top notch fits the message.

As an instance, at the same time as making an recognition speech for an award you can want to location at some point of the message that difficult paintings got you in that you are, at the identical time as acknowledging those who helped you alongside the manner. Going off of that, you may then select an anecdote that illustrates every those elements – say recounting a task you undertook with a few colleagues that delivered you acclaim and fulfillment.

You can also be invited to speak at an occasion without a selected topic, or one in which you're recommended to make one up of your very very personal. You can pick out a message first after which choose a tale that illustrates it, but some other opportunity is to head the opportunity manner spherical – you choose out a tale that you assume could be interesting to the target audience and fun to tell, then look at it to discover what training you may tack onto it.

Your message will manual you whilst selecting which factors of the story to emphasize – you ought to stay specifically on people who show your component. The problems you ought to make of which factors of the tale to location unique emphasis on are going to be looked at in the next step.

STEP 3: Work out your content material material

Having used your objective and message to choose out the story you want to tell, you may now want to tailor the content material of the tale for maximum impact. To start with, take some time to jot down down down the whole thing down exactly as you hold in thoughts it. If you have it in your journal this will be supremely smooth – just transcribing it and filling in a few info which you cannot have had been given down. At this point, your story is still quite raw – it's quite possibly interesting in its private right however you can need to refine it a piece to make it thrilling and attractive, in addition to to make certain that it puts at some point of your message effectively and is appropriate to the demographic of your target marketplace.

There are three elements to tinker with in this step – the situation, characters and information. We will check those for my part in turn.

The Situation

Now we get to some excessive crunchy elements – how do you assemble the situation of the tale to honestly captivate and the front your goal market? First and foremost, you need to tailor it to your target audience. It want to be something that is relatable to them – both some factor they've got or are experiencing or something they are able to preference or anticipate to take place to them. If your intention marketplace doesn't connect to your tale in some way then you haven't any desire of preserving their interest.

If you have got have been given a particular issue matter or are speak me to a specific form of crowd, then your art work in this situation is generally finished for you. Say, for example, you're invited to speak at a university for a careers day, you emphasize a few difficulty that has to do together with your studies and the academic and professional direction you had to take. If you are given the difficulty, you actually take the elements of the tale that examine and provide them prominence.

When you're speak me to a more generalized form of crowd, there are however some techniques you can tailor your story to them. There are a few universals of human experience we are able to all grow to be aware about with – falling in love, finding your calling, overcoming an obstacle – the listing is infinite. Drawing from this kind of will normally be a strong wager, however in case you want to be adventurous you could pass in advance and center your tale round some aspect that is greater unique and specialized to you. We additionally pay attention to tales to advantage new perspectives, so that you can talk approximately something precise on your gender, cultural enterprise organization, career or a few different affiliations that others out of doors of it could not ever revel in.

Simply having a common frame of reference amongst your story and your goal market isn't enough, despite the fact that. You are going to need a few components to hold them invested within the story and arrested sooner or later of. The wonderful tool you can use to gain that is tension. Regardless of the quantity of numerous emotions you set off for your goal marketplace, you could need there to be an element as a way to hold them guessing and seeking to recognize what's going to reveal up subsequent.

A proper deliver of that is warfare – having some factor this is retaining the critical parent of the story – be it you or someone else – from carrying out some element. To try this, u. S. The desired intention or give up-component near the start of the story. Have something that is thwarting or stopping that aim from being fulfilled, even supposing the struggle itself isn't the critical detail of the tale. It doesn't want to be a person in this antagonistic function – it's virtually incredible to try to avoid this due to the reality it may be visible as an attempt to slander that individual or carry yourself up by pushing them down –

nor does it ought to be implied to be a horrific component. The obstacle might also need to, for instance, be a heavy workload on a quick closing date, or a hassle that if solved would likely greatly assist plenty of people or a language barrier in a distant places land.

Conflict is also critical to reminiscences counseled with the purpose of being inspiring. People on occasion count on that this is unwanted on the equal time as telling a tale that is supposed to be motivational, that telling human beings approximately the hardships that lie earlier on a sure course will motive an audience to revel in disheartened. First of all, leaving out the hard factors of lifestyles in a tale can be considered as cheating or patronizing to the listener, and 2d of all it underestimates the tenacity of the human spirit. Human beings thrive in overcoming demanding situations, and telling humans of the hardships they will face on a outstanding route clearly motivates them to want to overcome that trouble themselves.

Characters

Clear, well-defined characters absolutely electricity a tale and offer it lifestyles, so you need to goal to extend the ones in your tale and purpose them to as colorful and sensible as possible.

Generally speaking, you could have a far more intimate fact of your characters than your target audience does. You will want to make sure you communicate that information to them. Be careful now not to succumb to the temptation to include as many info that describe them as viable and make the target marketplace apprehend every nuance of them as loads as you do. This is a mistake – taking too long putting in place your characters can consume precious time you may be the use of to advance the tale and motive your goal marketplace to float off. Besides, you'll in no manner have enough time to absolutely describe them truly, so that you shouldn't even try it.

What you need to do as an possibility is choose out or three inclinations that exceptional describe the individual, then pick one of those traits that certainly set them apart from the rest and emphasize it. Making the character stick inside the target market's minds and be smooth to differentiate from the rest is an extended way more critical than gaining an entire image of who they'll be as someone.

You ought to tie as a minimum one of the traits you pick out in together together with your message in a few manner, and within the case of the number one character you can need that characteristic to be the one you emphasize. You ought to additionally discover a manner to convey that function up within the tale. This will cement it in the minds of your goal marketplace, in addition supporting to imprint the character.

Many of the testimonies you tell will contain you as a person. You are, in spite of the whole lot, the top spectator in the reminiscences that display up on your lifestyles and you are the individual you know pleasant. Quite frequently you may truly be the best character inside the tale, with particular people referred to distantly or in passing and the majority of your interactions being with the situation. When telling a story in that you are a man or woman, don't overlook approximately that the equal factor that applies to unique characters applies to you: your target audience doesn't recognize you further to you do. Always dedicate the identical technique to describing yourself as you do your one of a kind character. Aim to painting yourself in a way that your target market can become aware of with which will sense associated with you – in case you are speak me to more younger humans, for example, talk about what you have been like when you have been their age (and no longer in a cantankerous "in my day" shape of way. Be sincere – you've got been simply as self-confident and carefree as they're).

Avoid portraying yourself as quality or praising yourself an excessive amount of. This can be seen as a sign of an overinflated ego, it certainly is off-setting to maximum human beings. Do be honest approximately your proper features, but aim to be a chunk self-deprecating. In unique, try to lower yourself in assessment with the target market a chunk in at the least one characteristic – in an wonderful-natured way, name yourself a few thing that most human beings can select out with and perhaps secretly suspect about themselves – lazy, scatterbrained or socially inept are a few correct examples. People like to be reminded that they are regular in having those traits and they are additionally going to be greater open to someone who isn't ideal like they'll be and indicates sufficient humility to well known that.

Detail

A quality story takes the identical technique to the details of the story installed because it does to characterization: it consists of absolutely sufficient to make the tale shiny and extremely good to the target audience however no longer plenty as to overburden them and make it tedious and dull.

Early on within the tale you will want to set the scene – describing the physical surroundings and/or the emotional context the characters are experiencing. The authentic necessities for this can be particular between a unmarried revel in and a drawn-out tale that spans a long time body. Generally, you will in truth should describe the physical and emotional context of a single state of affairs, while with an prolonged time body you may bypass the bodily if the story's content fabric is nice emotional or intellectual.

To illustrate this, if you are telling the story of the adventure you took to win an novice seashore volleyball championship, you could choose out to explain sure records like your workout court docket docket and climate situations or you can choose no longer to, however the maximum vital a part of the story is the desire and backbone you and your group felt as you rose thru the competition. When you are describing your very last in shape, however, you have to consist of data of the courtroom docket docket, the spectators and the organization sunglasses they had been sporting and the noise and chants they were making and so on, in addition to the exhilaration and anticipation you and your crew have been feeling.

As a cutting-edge rule, after the preliminary scene-placing each single element you supply the target market should emphasize your message and power the tale forward. Continuing with the instance of your seashore volleyball health's final healthful, you don't want to deliver an define of each unmarried player at the opposing component but you could describe their bruiser of a center-in advance who seemingly blocked almost all your volleys at the beginning, but you then definitely discovered her vulnerable component – an incapacity to dam whatever from left discipline – and started out out to take benefit of it to strength yourselves to victory.

Be conscious additionally that your goal marketplace isn't always you or your close friends you often change tales with. The tiny records that hobby you could not hobby them, so keep away from the temptation to encompass too quite some the ones.

STEP four: Structure your story

Stories have, because the earliest written documents we are able to find out, and for the duration of lots of cultures in some unspecified time in the future of the area observed a verified and constant form. Its near-ubiquity at some point of geography and time speaks volumes of its electricity and price. The shape that tales have located whilst you recollect that in all hazard the start of storytelling is the three problem shape: starting – center – quit. It works so properly because it's far logical and follows the styles we've placed in the natural global: the whole thing we take a look at this is problem to the glide of time, from the times and seasons to existence itself conforms to it.

Chapter 4: The Beginning

This is in which you seize the goal marketplace's creativeness and supply them the entirety they need to recognize to recognize the relaxation of the tale, so that you actually can't skimp on it. We've already touched on the contextual element you want to provide – genuinely sufficient, now not an excessive amount of – however you furthermore mght want to pay special interest to the opener.

What you could want is some issue to be able to right now snag the attention of the reader. In storytelling parlance this is known as a "hook" – a line or statement that right away units the stakes very immoderate. You start right within the movement – don't take the "Lord of the Rings" technique to starting your tale and start all of the way within the proverbial Shire, in advance than you've even set foot outside your home. Tolkien had the gain of the medium of print and 3 books over which to tell his tale. At absolute pleasant, you can have 15-20 minutes, most of the time far a great deal much less. If there are critical data that come earlier than the movement, you may inform them proper after the hook in a flashback.

To illustrate, say you are telling the tale of being misplaced in a huge metropolis even as you had been very more youthful, your message being the kindness of strangers. You don't begin alongside facet your mom telling you approximately the experience, discovered through the technique of packing up and getting ready, the lengthy stress there and the manner you drank manner an excessive amount of soda and needed to prevent the car to pee each 5 minutes until your mother truly cautioned you to pee in the empty Big Gulp cup you'll drank it from and so forth. You begin with a ambitious, to your face assertion like,

"There I modified into, a six 365 days antique U. S. Boy misplaced within the center of Manhattan and no longer the usage of a idea wherein my mom become".

The line is straight away arresting and adds to the tension with the resource of manner of creating the target market ask how you bought in that state of affairs inside the first area, it's an critical element which you can fill in by means of flashback right after – keeping to the crucial information, of course.

The center

This is the pork of the motion, and it's miles important that you maintain the stakes high eventually of. Being concise in records is particularly essential here – too many superfluous ones will wreck the float and deflate your story.

A fantastic manner of keeping the stakes excessive is thru strive-fail cycles – a ray of wish appears, elevating the goal market's expectancies only to have them upset at the same time as it seems to not quite be what they expected.

Using our example: you see a female dressed like your mom and run to her, but on closer inspections it seems no longer to be her. You think "she seems type, possibly I may want to ask her to help me," however it appears her English isn't exceptional. She one manner or the other figures out you're misplaced and buys you a candy bar to comfort you and subsequently reveals a policeman. She manages to speak with him that you're out of place and accompanies you with him to the police station to hold you employer and ensure you're solid. The police placed out a call for a mother missing her toddler. It's spoke back proper away, but it turns out to be some different woman searching out a few distinct little one actually…

The center is likewise in which you introduce questions which can be relevant in your message – need to you accept as true with this bizarre woman? Should you accept as true with the police? And so on.

The stop

This is in which you wrap the whole lot up, answer any questions you've raised and pressure domestic your ethical or message. You can pick out out to be diffused with this – permit your target audience to decide out what the tale must train them on their personal – or you could be direct and explicitly u . S. A. It. You can also leave your intention marketplace satisfied, or depart them hungering for extra by using way of manner of leaving a tidbit of every unique state of affairs following on out of your tale – as an example, your mother finally finds you after severa hours, the lady who helped you having stayed with you the complete time. You can permit that stand on its personal, or you may country the belief that there are right people obtainable you may consider, and you may pick out to tie the story off there or finish with the way you and your mom go out the station to find out that her vehicle, which she'd left idling via manner of the reduce returned in her rush to get to you is lengthy beyond…"but that's another story."

That very last approach is specially useful in case you've been speak me to a everyday purpose market and want to be invited once more, otherwise you need to be approached thru goal marketplace participants to inform them the possibility tale after the event

Telling your story: recommendations for the degree

Finally! We get to the bit in which you surely find out about what to do on the identical time because the time comes as a way to upward thrust up on diploma. The point of telling your tale is to hook up with the target market and call their lives, and irrespective of how suitable your actual tale is it is able to be undone by way of using a stupid normal overall performance at the stage. A notable on-degree presence, however, can surely make your tale, leaving it very well imprinted to your goal market's minds.

This bankruptcy will check how you can optimize your presence on the level through the usage of all the gadget you have got to be had to you.

Preparing for the quantity

Yes, there's however pretty a piece more instruction to do. The importance of education actually cannot be careworn sufficient, and the arrangements you have to make in particular for the diploma are pretty ruin away the ones you have to make at the identical time as writing out your story itself.

Commit your tale to memory

There is pretty loads extra to this that we'll sincerely test in element within the next economic catastrophe, however for now know-how that you need to do this is enough. You will now not want to read your tale wholesale off a web web page – that might be bulky and might significantly limit your interaction with the target market. You in fact don't need to inform your whole tale from memory in a rigid, truely rote manner both as that might nevertheless make your performance stiff, wood and lacking in character.

What you want to do is have an outline of your story – key points which you'll determine to reminiscence spherical which you could fill within the data. This leaves you especially flexible to paintings round your target marketplace's reactions and to be prepared for any situations alongside a while being reduce short because of walking behind schedule. With an outline, you received't be flustered thru a few component that comes up.

Optimally, your outline elements should be solidly imprinted on your memory so that you obtained't must lodge to cue playing cards. Working simplest off reminiscence gives you continue to more freedom to have interaction with and modify for your target market, so it genuinely is the super thing you can pick out to do. If you truly revel in like you may need them – you are however a newbie to this whole public talking problem or you suspect you may become flustered or scatterbrained – then it can be OK a great way to apply them. Write out your outline points on small quantities of card or stiff-sponsored paper in a size that you can look at from arm's length — you don't need to need to look at them seeking to decipher what you've written. If your handwriting looks as if a person dipped a spider in ink and permit it cross wild for your cue card, you'd as an opportunity print them out. All the same, strive to discuss with your cue gambling cards as low as feasible and try to wean yourself from them as time goes on.

Your talking engagement may additionally additionally additionally definitely have a call for banning the use of cue playing cards, rendering the element settled and forcing you to rely on your reminiscence by myself besides.

Check out your venue

The next problem you want to do is get to recognize the statistics of your venue. Will there be a level or will you be telling your tale from in the crowd? How will the group be positioned — seated in rows or at tables? Will there be a lectern a superb manner to face in the decrease returned of or now not? What are the physical dimensions of the gap you'll be in and the scale of the gang? The data of your venue will dictate exactly the manner you execute the rest of your everyday performance. If feasible, discover a manner to get inside the venue – putting yourself inside the actual speaking vicinity will offer you with a sincere higher idea of the manner to optimize your performance to it.

Get your look proper

When the night time of your actual speech comes, you may must take account of your physical look. This will once more in massive detail be dictated thru using the context of the occasion – if it's a professional occasion, you'll ought to located on formal garb (till you work for a hip startup or tech enterprise in which you could placed on jeans and a tee shirt), if you're the high-quality guy or maid of honor at a pal's wedding ceremony you'll be sporting a few component themed tuxedo or get dressed has been decided on for you. For most sports in which you're actually telling your story that don't have a get dressed code you can put on something you commonly placed on in public – you do need to reveal off who you're. Avoid wearing distracting apparel, even though – over-incredible styles and shades, dangly earrings, accessories like hats and sun sunglasses and so on. They may additionally moreover draw attention on your look but they draw it far from the content material of what you are announcing.

Chapter 5: Warm Up In Advance Than Getting On Degree

Before you bodily get onto the stage, you want to warmness yourself up and get your thoughts primed to it. You ought to have complete control over your frame at the same time as you are on degree as we will see afterward, so that you ought to prepare your body as properly. It's an extremely good idea to have a complete pre-diploma ritual which you undertake each time you're about to move up that gets you into the proper frame of mind. Meditation is a extremely good vicinity to start for this – there are hundreds of techniques you may use, discover the best that works for you. You can also do stretches and breathing carrying sports, in addition to vocal warmness-united statesto prepare your voice for the subsequent few minutes in that you'll be the use of it constantly.

Connecting alongside your aim market

This is honestly important if you want to effectively get your message at some stage in.

The intention market has to enjoy a unique bond with you, in order that your emotions grow to be their feelings too and you take them along aspect you as you plunge into the sector of your story.

Be your self

This piece of advice is repeated everywhere in recent times nearly to the factor of being trite, however it's miles no much less real for that. The individual you're is the pleasant who professional and created the tale, so your telling may be plenty greater right in case you permit your person to polish through.

Maintain eye touch

Eye touch is of important importance at the same time as you're on level. The eyes are the window to the soul, as they're announcing, and your audience will better hook up with your emotions in case you keep direct touch with their eyes. There's an vintage public talking tip that asserts you ought to look someplace just over the heads of the target marketplace, especially in case you are fearful. The inefficacy of this evasive tactic in addressing the issues inside the returned of anxiety can be looked at in the next bankruptcy, however it's additionally very obvious to an target marketplace at the identical time as you are retaining off their gaze. Look at them proper now at eye diploma, catching the gaze of person folks that're in the direction of you at random an amazing manner to experience proper away connected to you.

Another gain of retaining eye contact is that you could maintain watch on the target marketplace's reactions. This way you could gauge how they're reacting to what you're saying and adapt consequently. Remember that your target marketplace is not you – you may have superb tale elements which you have protected definitely so they may elicit a particular response from them. They may also react to them in any other manner – a humorous tale you belief is probably a killer ought to probable handiest elicit some chuckles, while every special which you idea wasn't that applicable may additionally moreover cause them to snigger quite hard. The equal may match for every other emotional reactions you need to elicit. This is wherein that flexibility given thru going off an define in fact comes in to be had – you may then regulate your speech on the fly to hit the ones factors that resonate with the target audience.

Your voice and tone

Your voice goes to be the number one way you get your data at some point of – you use it to transmit the real terms of your tale, of route. It's therefore definitely vital that you get the nuances of the usage of it on diploma just proper.

Volume and enunciation

To start with, you want to make sure that you are heard. The quantity and projection of your voice are quite crucial proper here. This is in which casing your venue in advance simply is available in to be had, so you will be prepared: if there can be a public address system, you then actually'll be blanketed, however if there isn't you will want to take account of the scale of the venue so that you can project your voice to benefit the members of the goal market farthest from you.

The articulation of your terms is also very vital. You must make certain your words aren't muddled and every syllable can be without issue and clearly heard and avoid mumbling. You need to avoid speakme too speedy and speak with a measured tempo just so your target audience can in fact pay hobby what you are saying.

Tone

Speak virtually and conversationally – the way you may normally talk with someone face-to-face, great adjusting your quantity as vital to obtain absolutely everyone. Whatever feelings you are attempting to awaken, gain this with the identical tone of voice you will with one on one. Speaking conversationally is every different manner to connect with your target market — it creates a sense of familiarity among you and them.

Use your voice to create atmosphere

Now, the above elements are virtually pointers, the rules that shape the foundation of your vocal location. The fact is that your voice is an brilliant device that you could use to steer the feelings of your audience and upload weight in the returned of your phrases.

We'll start with tone — there are styles of story wherein it's miles suitable to magnify your tone far from its natural cadence. These are commonly people-kind memories — legends, fairytales and so on. You need to decide to tell your personal tale this manner for impact; however your functionality as a storyteller might must be quite superior to pull it off. Don't try and do it at a right occasion on the same time as you're nonetheless building your potential, but you can test with it with a small, supportive organization like your buddies or storytelling club that may give you feedback over whether or not or not or no longer you're doing it properly.

Playing spherical along with your extent, pitch and pace are extra routine – they fall inside the magnificence of the usage of your herbal voice as you in all likelihood use them each day. Use them to feature any other length of drama into your story – improve your voice and pitch and communicate quicker to create delight and decrease them to create gravity or suspense.

Silence

In all your talking, you want to by no means underestimate the electricity of silence. Its first use want to be simply while you upward thrust up to talk or enter the degree. After any applause and cheering have died down, pause for a 2nd earlier than launching into your tale. You'll be aware that this is a few element every expert public speaker does, from presidents and politicians to stand up comedians, tv hosts and additional. This 2d of silence has benefits for you and your intention market: it gives you an opportunity to acquire your mind, take a deep breath and start your story strongly, and it allows the target marketplace to loosen up and be organized to take in your message.

You should furthermore use pauses within the frame of your story. These serves two features: to begin with, it offers you an opportunity to seize your breath and set up your thoughts in advance than transferring on, and secondly it leaves region for goal market reactions – have planned silences in locations in that you count on the goal market to react audibly, which incorporates laughter for jokes, gasps for marvel, 'aww's for commiseration or adorable moments or applause in that you discovered it is able to acquire. As already noted, those won't hit in that you count on them to, so adjust your gaps consequently. Allowing the audience's reactions to run their course lets in them to experience their feelings to their fullest amount and additionally makes effective your entire story may be heard as you received't be attempting to talk above them and that they received't however be hung up on a element you have were given moved on past.

You also can use silence for emphasis, and to allow the target market time to soak up a specifically deep or complex problem that they may not be capable of way absolutely if you don't offer them that point.

Your frame and mannerisms

You have to hold in thoughts that the target market ought to have its eyes on you – their consciousness isn't always only on what you are announcing however in your physical presence as well. You must use that in your advantage, the use of your frame to speak through emphasizing and accentuating your story, and must keep away from sure behaviors that in reality distract and detract from your tale.

As a primary tenet, just like pretty some the recommendation already given, bring yourself the identical on level as you do in real life and keep away from overdoing subjects or being overly theatrical.

Your facial expressions

It's absolutely essential to take examine of these as they may be the maximum prominent non-verbal way to talk your feelings. As a preferred rule, you need to located on a pleasant, sociable smile while you're telling your tale. If the issue of your tale swings enormous on each thing on the dimensions of emotion, then you can undertake a base facial function extra in step with it – grave for a extra somber tale and extra excited for a lighter, funnier story. Your story might also have upswings and downswings of emotion, even though – modify your expressions to go along with them.

Your fingers

These are every other splendid tool for highlighting components of your story. How you operate them will depend upon whether you've got were given a lectern or not – in case you do, then spending most of the story with them resting on it will do wonderful, but you continue to do need to skip them a bit. Raise, wave and clench your arms as critical to animate components of your story. If you do no longer have a lectern, there are two extra possibilities: both you have a microphone otherwise you do no longer or also can have a stalk or bead microphone. Whatever the case is it only in reality affects the huge form of palms you want to address – a stick microphone will occupy one in each of your arms complete-time. Whichever is real, you ought to avoid definitely leaving your free hand(s) to keep thru your aspect. Use them for emphasis, or to demonstrate.

Your posture

Avoid slouching. Everything about you on degree ought to exude self belief.

Move!

If you're on an open degree, keep away from spending too much time rooted to at the least one spot. Don't flow into spherical too much, every – it is able to wind up being distracting. What you must do is pick a niche at kind of the center of the extent, and each few moments take a few steps to the left, wait a few moments, and then take every other few steps to the proper, forming a small, difficult orbit spherical that spot. If you've got have been given a lectern, the want to transport round is taken from you, and also you won't honestly must do it if your speak me function is inside the crowd each.

Practice

Practice is past essential In perfecting your story for the diploma. Yes, technically it's far part of getting equipped on your basic overall performance, but there are additives to it that by means of manner of the usage of necessity need to test with matters we mentioned in the previous financial ruin, and it has to return after it right here in order that they may be looked at in context.

You need to apply your exercising to check with numerous methods, gain self guarantee and perfect your tale. We will check the three maximum crucial elements of exercise and what they entail. Practice anywhere and everywhere – some of the elements given could require precise settings and topics to be present, however they will be now not essential honestly all of the time. Practice whenever you have got the time.

1. Practice!

Of course this is the primary and maximum critical problem you need to do – absolutely workout your speech. It isn't always going to be sufficient simply to recite it for your head – you'll must do it out loud. There are some benefits to education your tale aloud: to begin with, you'll get used to genuinely the use of your voice to inform your story. The enjoy of talking out your story is pretty extremely good from going thru it mentally, and you'll ought to acclimatize yourself to it so you aren't honestly encountering it for the primary time while you get on degree.

The 2nd advantage is genuinely tied to this identical reality: there are wonderful phrases and terms that may sound proper whilst you consider them but won't be so exquisite at the same time as spoken out loud. There will also be some turns of word which may be inadvertent tongue-twisters – poetically picturesque and fascinating however tough to pronounce well. You may additionally moreover furthermore want to take them on as a venture, but it's far great to try to hold your phrases simple, particularly if you are in reality beginning out.

You additionally don't speak at the equal price as you think. Actually taking the time to say your tale out loud permits you to gauge some time lots higher. It additionally lets you diploma how saying your story aloud honestly makes you revel in – there can be additives that are greater emotional whilst you absolutely communicate them out, and also you don't want to be blindsided via them.

Finally, it also facilitates you start to decide out any technical issues you can have together with your shipping – a machine on the way to preserve within the direction of as you provide your tale.

You can begin via reading your story out as you have got were given written it in complete, but as you go through more than one repetitions, start to work out on telling it from your define. Graduate from the whole story to plenty a lot much less-genuine bullet factors, then in your define and ultimately to disposing of these truly. You may additionally moreover nonetheless want to have them with you on stage if you can, virtually as a backup however optimally you must reason to have the potential to inform your tale via heart.

Do your exercising repute up – specially if that is how you'll be telling the story at the night of the event itself. This will higher assist you get into the headspace you will need to be in come tale night time time, and being seated additionally alters your body structure and voice projection. You ought to additionally exercise the real actions you recommend on making at the degree, in an effort to assist you extend muscle-reminiscence that is in sync alongside your phrases.

You want to furthermore assignment to exercise inside the putting you may be in while you are making the speech. If you're able to get into the actual venue, then that is probably stellar. Otherwise, content material material yourself with seeking to recreate it as nice you may through locating a similar vicinity. Most vital is to recreate the actual degree format – attempt to use a place that has comparable dimensions with the stage. If you'll have a lectern, find out one to exercising with, and if you'll have a microphone locate one, otherwise use a in addition sized cylindrical item.

2. Observe your self

It's frequently not feasible to determine exactly how you could look or sound to every other man or woman, so it's vital to try to get an concept of the way you appear from the out of doors. One thing you could do to obtain that is to exercise inside the front of a replicate. Being able to certainly see yourself will help you amazing the physical factors of your typical performance. Pay particular hobby to your posture, facial features and gestures to peer how a person else may check them.

You need to additionally make audio recordings of yourself delivering the tale. Your voice is specifically hard to gauge the sound of outside your head due to the fact your ears revel in the resonance given with the beneficial resource of your skull. No one loves to concentrate recordings in their voice in the beginning, but you can get used to it and be better able to select out whether or not you are the usage of it proper after a few initial listens. Once you do get used to it you may be better capable of because it ought to be gauge and adjust your volume, pitch, tone and pace to the maximum greatest degrees. You may also be higher able to find those phrases and phrases that sound a bit off or you couldn't quite enunciate properly. It can also be a beneficial device for assisting you internalizes the story – thru paying attention to it again and again it's far going to stick in your mind an entire lot higher.

You can integrate the essence of the two above thoughts through making video recordings of yourself turning in the speech. A video works even better than a replicate because you can in fact evaluation yourself without the concurrent stress and distraction of looking to recall and tell your story, and it may offer you with a view that someone else must genuinely have. Making recordings of your self isn't always in any respect tough in recent times you don't want cinematic splendid – your Smartphone's mic and camera will do just top notch.

3. Get feedback

As a good buy because of the truth the preceding element offers you an outside perspective, you could probable though have a few blind spots about yourself and your not unusual performance. You will want other minds to check your ordinary performance and provide you with an out of doors mindset on it. Find a check target market to inform your tale to, ideally one this is of the same demographic as your actual audience.

It isn't without a doubt encouragement you are searching out proper here: ask for sincere and specific comments on their thoughts of the tale, the way it made them experience, what factors of your trendy overall performance located them off, specifics on your look and voice and typically how you can enhance. Having an target audience may additionally even assist you get used to actually appearing in the front of different people, which may be very one in every of a kind from appearing to a wall or empty room.

Chapter 6: Overcoming Fear And Mastering To Like The Level

Fear of public speaking is one of the most common fears, ranking above such phobias as heights, spiders or maybe lack of existence. Chances are you are one of the billions who proportion this worry or maybe in case you aren't, hold analyzing, you never recognize while you may be of assist to any individual.

To apprehend worry of public speak me permit's check its roots – it's a fear of failure and making a fool of oneself in the the front of a crowd, which may additionally reason a loss in social fame and the following knock to at least one's capacity to woo a mate. The irony is, of direction, that it's frequently the priority itself that reasons failure through using attractive the primitive "fight or flight" response, which diverts belongings far away from the wondering colleges and causes bodily tics.

A lot of nicely-due to this humans have attempted to advocate "remedies" to this worry. No doubt you've heard the recommendation to appearance above the aim market's heads, wear a fortunate allure, remind yourself it will quick be over or to assume the goal marketplace bare. All of those have one thing in not unusual: they are primarily based on avoidance – taking your mind off the priority or getting the enjoy over with. This is NOT beneficial – the concern will typically nonetheless be there and inflicting its undesirable outcomes.

What an outstanding treatment for worry need to do is manipulate the worry at the same time as it arises instead of avoid it, and ultimately triumph over it certainly so it is no longer an problem. You want to learn how to prevent fearing the diploma, and as an opportunity to embody and love it.

An crucial query to ask while you pay interest any piece of recommendation: what does it accumulate? Does it masks the worry or assist me manage and conquer it? Ask the equal question for any behavior you discover yourself doing whilst you are worried. It want to no longer genuinely cover or distract from your fear but it need to help you overcome it.

We are going to observe what you want to do in the route of 3 levels of time: training, getting at the diploma and the aftermath.

1. Preparation

Hold on in your hat, because of the truth what I am about to inform you is going to blow your mind: the maximum important issue you could do within the route of schooling as a manner to relieve your worry is PRACTICE! Following the stairs given inside the preceding monetary disaster will do absolute wonders in yourself guarantee – you'll get to understand your fabric interior and out, workout any bugs that can cause you to unnecessarily stumble and get snug with the venue and the concept of talking to a crowd.

There are a pair more topics you could try this moreover call once more to preceding chapters: take storytelling commands as they will decorate your ultra-modern competencies, and the assure of know-how is a outstanding booster of self guarantee. Talking approximately some difficulty you're obsessed on moreover permits, so tying your tale in with a message that has a deep effect on you and that you actually need to percentage with others is a excellent idea.

2. on the extent

Eliminating your fear at the degree moreover starts right in advance than you in truth arise to talk. Having a pre-overall overall performance ritual is a first-rate concept, one which even the masters observe. Tailor it to your self – you may stretch, perform a few easy bodily sports or meditate. If you continue to have a few traumatic energy, use this time to refocus it into excitement – worry and anticipation every percentage the equal hormonal pathway, and all it takes from you is a powerful mindset that sees what is coming for the possibility it's far and no longer as a trial to be suffered.

When you get on degree, be aware of your breathing. It is simply easy to overlook to respire properly. Use your deliberate moments of silence to take a truly deep breath that clears your lungs. Breathing deeply receives more oxygen to the thoughts, sharpening your recognition and flushing out the priority-inflicting hormones.

Keep all the hints given within the fourth economic disaster in thoughts, specifically averting speakme too rapid. Rushing will purpose you to stumble, if you need to add on your tension.

3. Afterwards

When the entirety is over, take some time to recognize your achievement earlier than you get into assessment mode. Don't be grateful that it's over, be thankful that you obtain to tell your story, and if you did have a few anxiety be proud which you encountered it head-on. Remember the immoderate best reactions and the times you bought the institution to react the manner you desired them to.

Once you've completed that, recognize the aftermath due to the fact the prelude in your next engagement and start to awareness your energies on that. Treat any errors you may have made as a analyzing enjoy and goal to do higher subsequent time. The real event itself is extensively amazing from each little bit of workout you have were given accomplished as plenty as that factor, so if you may get hold of a recording of your real common performance and examine that. Look for areas you need to decorate and exercising for the subsequent time you tell a tale with them in mind.

With this form of mindset, you may begin to assume the sensation of success that includes appearing on degree and in advance than you recognize it, all worry might be long past, changed through a using preference to get up and tell greater testimonies.

Chapter 7: What Is Powerful Storytelling?

Powerful Storytelling has been one of the unique darlings of the advertising and corporate worldwide. It's a advertising and advertising tactic that has built it from the corridors of energy to mom and pa shops anywhere within the business enterprise international. Over the subsequent decade, storytelling is even regarded because of the truth the single most influential enterprise functionality. Throughout the subsequent decade, effective storytelling is even viewed because the most powerful corporation information. This eBook is set the implementation of a structure for telling a tale, a justification for the usage of narratives to sell manipulate, and guidelines and strategies to beautify the managers ' functionality to percent memories. It might also encompass:

The powerful storytelling triangle

Tensive conflicts and meanings

Bridging characters and target market

Emotional arc and empathy to draw the target audience

Ways for the model of storytelling on a company degree

The need for storytelling in groups

The key elements

Constructive version of sense making

The real-life worrying conditions

The video video games and tips

The unique tones

Creative limits

Storytelling - A Beautiful Art!

Active and effective storytelling is a lovable art work. A properly-advanced and well-provided narrative will break down limitations of developing old and hold interest and entice the target marketplace. Stories are recollected and remembered prolonged after special orations. Understanding the fundamentals of storytelling and incorporating them will increase the recollections. Narrating a story is an aptitude and abilities that cannot really be picked up perusing one medium placed up by means of a bit child that loves branding. It is an capability which you need to make investments greater energy — and further assets — on getting to know and recounting to higher memories, specifically as it identifies with building and growing convincing ads for brands.

Like you probable heard, each logo has it's far one in each of a kind tale. How you tell yours, will effect your crowd's response and thusly have an impact for your piece of the general company. Therefore, crafting an fun and attractive tale during the emblem you need to marketplace may be very vital. As increasingly more groups recognize that narrative is critical to solving masses of present day center control troubles and key traumatic conditions – collectively with articulating the risks and opportunities found by way of way of government manage gear which incorporates strategic goals, situation assessment, predicament resolution, and quandary goals – the question turns into: how does a CEO use storytelling efficiently? But executives and leaders who are instinctively storytelling revolutionary additionally want to comprehend a manner to tailor their storytelling method to the precise hassle the employer faces.

Although the need to teach executives and commercial enterprise representatives to use suave narration to encourage and direct their company to reply correctly to those aggressive demanding situations is substantially understood by way of the usage of the usage of essential organizations, the fact is that most groups want help in getting the complete advantage of making use of the paintings of storytelling. A close to emphasis and sharp attention want to be maintained on the corporation reason being accompanied with the method even as implementing storytelling, in addition to at the particular narrative patterns, styles, and genres associated with one-of-a-type uses. A a success CEO uses an emotional narrative about the vision of the enterprise to extend operations, attraction to buyers and companions, set lofty goals and encourage employees.

As a pacesetter describes a story, they are now not best helping their group makes revel in of the annoying situations, they're furthermore infusing them with context – addressing what is critical, what corporation dreams are or what they represent to the crew and their leader on a private degree and practical level.

This eBook explores elite employer professions through the twin prism of sense-making and creativeness, as referred to in interviews with company and company leaders in life-information. This examines how their observations and reviews of growing their jobs within and throughout massive corporations make feel, narrativize and legitimize. Most of the time, a well-made tale can also additionally even alternate an apparently hopeless condition into an surprising triumph.

Stories precise beliefs and feelings and might display similarities and variations between the views of human beings. Elucidating man or woman stories includes sharing that could assist form bonds and robust systems. With pondered photograph, those can create versatility to increase durability via contemplation.

Several other human beings expect the narration clashes in a few way with truth. In this opinion, the genuine storyteller is a spinner of yarns that entertains without honestly being grounded. Powerful Storytelling might not contradict reality. It's usually crafted at the integrity of the story and its teller within the business organization international and some one of a kind vicinity. There is continuously a bond implied a few of the storyteller and his visitors. This calls for a pledge to meet the goals of the aim marketplace, when they had been aroused. The target audience volunteers their time to the storyteller, knowledge he will use it for them efficiently. Time is the scarcest asset for max commercial enterprise humans; the storyteller who disrespects it'll pay dearly. Each storyteller is in the business business enterprise of expectations-control and need to take responsibility for successfully guiding audiences thru the experience of memories combining each suspense and fulfillment.

Authenticity and integrity is a key feature of the storyteller. He desires to be in alignment together with his tale — his lips, foot, and arms need to circulate in the equal course. A effective storyteller is privy to his very very personal maximum profound features and uncovers them in his tale with genuineness and realism.

An approach to storytelling

Businesses step by step understand the importance and relevance of an approach to storytelling as a expertise in management and management. In a time whilst representatives want a greater prominent feeling of direction and significance from artwork, the recollections that a corporation shares – wherein it's been, wherein it is going, what its issues are – aren't just subtle techniques of speaking facts, they may be an incentive for personnel to attach and encourage.

The approach inside the direction of storytelling is firmly related with techniques, techniques, and gadget, as an example, Most Critical Change, Contextual investigations, and Photo Voice. Stories offer sudden insights and display esoteric records. It pushes choice-makers in methods which are without a doubt now not possible for quantitative numbers, figures, and reviews. Storytelling will bring feelings In more element and supply an reason behind issues greater efficaciously than conventional achievement reporting.

Storytelling method is an exceptional method of human articulation and expressions that assists in making experience with detecting of the past and in comprehending capability opportunities. While it is an ancient exercise to get collectively to percentage recollections, exams regularly make use of personal narratives via one-of-a-type storytelling strategies to get expertise approximately the impact of boom tasks.

Eight Tracks to figuring out an approach to storytelling:

There are 8 one-of-a-kind tracks towards the strategic approach of storytelling.

1. THE CHARACTER'S PERSONA:

Find the characters within the returned of a tale the characters that pressure the trouble. You cannot most effective label an man or woman but additionally a location, an occurrence, even a form.

Chapter 8: The Descriptive And Referential Segment:

Show audiences why some factor does seem or occur and the manner it abilities.

3. FAQ AND TRENDING PATTERNS OF STORIES:

Question yourself if you want to research or remember a broader image. Trends aren't associated absolutely to the environment or cultural ancient beyond; speak about crook hobby or economic device.

4. INVESTIGATIVE ANALYSIS:

Look at misconduct, "follow the money," test political struggles or rivalries and employ the statistics and statistics to be had.

5. MONOLOGUE:

A narrative of personalities, situations, excitement, and anxiety.

6. LIFETIME SUMMARY OR SOMETHING DESCRIPTIVE:

This issue will alter the depth and tone and anxiety; provide the panoramic images that shape the backdrop and context for the movement; cryptic recommendations, endorse motives; illustrate sentiment and frame of thoughts in both character and reader.

7. THE PERSPECTIVE STORY:

In a completely precise manner, make human beings inform a tale: Q&A, panel dialogue, a line of statements, or brief evocative description.

Eight THE VIRTUAL SIDE:

The top notch way to technique some memories is through snap shots, seen consequences or illustrations.

In the organization sectors, there may be a declare that enterprise alternatives are dictated simply on evidence and explanation is a fallacy. Individuals make the choices at every buy (even in B2B), now not groups. But effective shipping of the tale is what motivates humans to make choices. Stories have a frequent capacity to persuade behavioral trade and manipulate conduct. Whether you are a shop clerk, an IT pro or even a C-suite exec, exquisite memories in no way overlook approximately to spellbind.

Another perfect approach for corporation leaders and business executives is to steer purchasing choices and behaviors, tell an tremendous story that influences the emotions of your target marketplace. Here are some strategies to get you going.

1. PERSONIFICATION OF NARRATIVE:

Obviously, humans are probably to companion themselves with individuals over fictional characters. So one manner to invoke compassion and understanding to your target marketplace is to have characters with which they may be capable of identify-or possibly better. Nicely-superior goal identification is crucial here. For crafting your tale, create a ' hero ': a man or woman with indistinguishable attributes and pains from that of the character. That technique is first-class for illustrating movies in which you can highlight your suitable or provider as a manual for the hero's adventure.

Not every piece of your content material cloth must be pedagogic. Indirectly precise thoughts, and positioned a few pride into them. Offer a provider or software rather than a bodily product and question the target market like what if it became behaving like someone? Content that circulates across the intention market is short and eccentric. Viral content is typically brief and unconventional- i.E. Shareable-kind. If brand photo and interest is your primary problem, start via taking your content material cloth cloth with analogies and metaphors for a soar.

2. SHARE YOUR ALTERNATIVES OF AUDIENCE CHALLENGES:

The option to ' worry, confusion, and doubt ' furthermore exhibits a gap. Show a worst-case situation and all are listening. Identify the worrying situations and strain spots the organization faces upfront to attract their recognition. Then exhibit how your products or services can assist to manage up with the problems.

3. THE DATA-DRIVEN STORIES:

Begin with empirical data and records to hold your tale the more ' punch. 'It improves accuracy and adds energy in your situation, which hits the rational 1/2 of of the brains of business enterprise preference-makers.

4. JOURNEY AND DRAMATIC ARC:

Try to take your target market on a journey because every now and then a adventure consists of sufficient of a dramatic arc which the story shows itself. Histories of the financial corporation are suitable for this approach. Tell the story about your company – the way it improved from scratch, conquered disturbing situations and benefited customers.

5. THE GAME OF POWERFUL CONTENT:

Finally, reminiscences might also speak in your crowd's inherent feelings, but its outward inspirations like non-forestall manipulate recognition and remunerates that preserve them locked in. This is mainly applicable for Millennial, on the side of many that raised up with video Video video games and cash back rewards in colleges. The idea of a hobby in powerful content is the version of exercise wondering to indulge and treatment the audience's traumatic conditions. Only multiple examples are showing real-time outcomes of the survey or ballot , making the films immersive or designing exercise-like conditions that empower the site visitors.

6. THE RULES TO BREAK:

There's one further approach that of certainly no method the least bit. There are only guidelines if it pertains to the modern content. Pursue them for a beginning but don't be scared if critical to break far from the norm. Try out new era to figure out new techniques of storytelling.

The tale teller's wheel

Stories have lubed the wheels of mankind for decades. Stories had been carried out as a way of disseminating tactical records and techniques for uncovering strategic statistics. The shared fireside paved the manner for this human interaction, and the diffusion of data, conceiving a massive milestone in human history.

The path to the cultural identity of cooperative organization isn't easy and natural. Storytellers have an duty to keep the narrative intact at some point of each diploma of the adventure. Consistency enhances the tale's tone, which gives credence. It is especially vital while the corporation's story is told to its employees; you ought to persuade or win in the course of the personnel so that everybody is conscious the goal and everybody realizes what the business business agency is willing to do or attain.

The storyteller's wheel is the expertise of the conceptual framework of Yarning and Aboriginal storytelling.

Aboriginal storytelling

Concept and framework of yarning/Aboriginal storytelling

Yarning storytelling is an vital a part of Aboriginal society's methods and shape. Stories are appealing and rising, supplying access to layers of profound social and actual statistics that make up the social and cultural character of Aboriginal human beings. Storytelling is regularly related to ' yarning ' for severa Aboriginal humans, wherein humans congregate informally to lighten up and draw on new or historical statistics tales.

The conceptual framework of yarning storytelling is moreover about innovation and creativity, it's miles the area humans be a part of up to percent statistics through retelling, re-displaying and making new recollections through new encounters, new human beings and new places. Significant own family statistics and antique testimonies are parodied in new and innovative strategies as a tool to deliver a deeper recognize-the way to the smarter contributors of the organization or the organizations who although ought to take a look at their sociocultural identity. The framework moreover includes expert use of voice, speech and body language, rhythm, use of seen symbolism, facial, due to this, creation of the plot and man or woman, the natural tempo of narration, and meticulous proper reminiscence.

Chapter 9: Storytelling And Severa Worldwide

Storytelling is a crucial phenomenon to all geographical regions, societies, and ideologies. Stories are capable of transcending demographic groups, cultures, and genders and attracting listeners ' creativity and interest no matter records.

Internal and outdoor administrative center variety, the enhancements in generation and imperatives of global undertaking make the venture of enhancing administrative verbal exchange wider than ever. The narrative model or the precept of "storytelling" has been proposed as an crucial intercultural verbal exchange technique inside the numerous international.

Storytelling in a numerous international is the notion that it fills the severa correspondence needs of the existing heterogeneous workforce. This introduces a storytelling paradigm as a entire agency communique device, explores how storytelling may be used effectively inside the complicated artwork environment and gives severa opportunities for added increase and growth.

Stories construct a bridge of correspondence that pals the left and right components of the thoughts via addressing logical and rational elements, virtually as an person's passionate factors, emotional objectives, and targets. In the agency location, storytelling is normally applied in selling and product improvement. This method can be used to decorate consequences in many distinct fields too. The pass-cultural conversation is one of the best spots to apply the storytelling. The concept of range in storytelling is a way to engage with a bilingual and multicultural group due to the fact reminiscences will decorate dreams and priorities in your marketplace. Stories bind and comprise human beings; they deliver context to our messages and assemble emotional ties amongst human beings.

Globalization has come to be the trademark of the prevailing technology. Culturally various connections are developing extensively inside the work environment in addition to in our regular lives, and, obviously, in our community. However, due to language barriers, limitations and social contrasts, and correspondence between humans having one-of-a-kind backgrounds have a tendency to provide some misconceptions. Misconception takes location while someone tries to narrate a tale approximately his / her neighborhood life-style to human beings from other worldwide places and does now not comprehend the listener may additionally moreover view the story in a super manner. In your neighborhood way of life, the identical tale might not yield the identical consequences as you forecast. But that does not advocate we haven't any options to misconceptions. Through pertaining to our very private memories and converting our impressions of these stories we can also obtain shared understandings. At instances, we also can give you bad feedback and feedback as funny, ridiculous or every so often even unreasonable even as we've got were given a have a look at something incredible from our neighborhood way of existence. Most of these distortions are oblivious due to the fact our cultural historical past is equipping each one people with included blinders, hid and implicit assumptions and assertions that govern our questioning.

The concept of range also indicates how way of life can effect how humans reply to a tale, no longer actually the cloth of a plot, however the aesthetic fashion of storytelling among specific cultures. That trivial nuance is wonderful in films and books, and is also fantastic on how entrepreneurs conduct their interaction techniques and conversation techniques whilst it relates to cultural advertising and marketing. Diversity via storytelling is the essence of tradition. It is how facts is conveyed, how rituals are expressed and the manner customs are endemic to a network. The not unusual way of existence is set up in a mutual convention of conveying. The tales a collective tells to precise what ideals and requirements society holds. But it isn't in reality what testimonies we need to supply to the tradition to relay, it is how they pick out to tell them. Are they getting to the aspect? Do they persist with specifics? What is the significance of context vs outcomes?

Each parents examines the world in a completely unique prism. Our accrued lifestyles memories, our gender, and racial origins, and our private convictions decide that prism. It is what paperwork the manner we get the arena and revel in this. We are human beings, and thru default, we are gravitating to fantastic recollections portrayed by the use of way of excellent storytellers. Thus, extra frequently than now not, our notion systems may be in element customary by means of the usage of using every different, extra metaphorical, digital camera's lens — and the storyteller on the opportunity fringe of that lens. Yet on the identical time as there are uniformities and diversities in the back of the prism, we grow to believe that the picture portrayed to us via using this universe is the most effective one: a view from the dominant manner of lifestyles' attitude. A universe wherein replicated, restricted, and misinformed imagery can regularly bring about the stereotyping and prejudice of those much less-represented, impacting us an extended way more than we understand. The worldwide can be a higher place if there may be a greater diverse network of storytellers and trouble areas to inform us reminiscences through their lenses. Once we've got got variety in the back of the lens — impacting casting, and scripts, documentary situation subjects, and problems — a better percentage of narrators can see themselves on display screen and in memories that provide opportunity strategies to the dominant narrative.

The attitude of Corporate Storytelling

Corporate storytelling is the workout of constructing a imaginative and prescient that introduces a brand new attitude or reinforces a factor of view or movement through the use of memories of people, the organization the past, expectancies for the future, social bonding and the interest itself.

Corporate storytelling may be an intellectually stimulating and powerful mechanism of internal public members of the own family. The attributes of internal storytelling make it a great method for an organization to attach more successfully with its employees and enhance employee loyalty. Corporate storytelling consists of the usage of storytelling as a viable tool for internal verbal exchange and employee engagement, a critical characteristic of organizational public circle of relatives' people that would create client take delivery of as proper with and boom the identification and photo of the organization This method folks that are extra dedicated and have a immoderate degree of trust, as their boss is extra vulnerable to feeling buoyant closer to their general overall performance and act constructively, which could emerge as strong inner and outside reputations.

The use of company memories as an organizational PR communication approach will enhance humans ' opportunities of turning into champions of their business enterprise. Internal PR, that encompasses the improvement of commercial enterprise organization-employee interactions, pertains to the strategic approach of maintaining organization-employee relationships that cause keeping properly sufficient organizational engagement, morale, and efficiency. This includes the tactical use of notable in internal communication to teach personnel on resources, aid structures, and corporation values.

A corporate memory which is probably targeted on developing employee engagement with the identity of the agency are a achievement at enhancing inner organizational loyalty. This electricity of mind performs a key characteristic in an company's recognition, every internally and externally, through growing employee satisfaction with the logo values and requirements. This also can possibly result in better interplay of stakeholders, as more engaged and inspired humans come to be storytellers to functionality stakeholders on behalf in their company.

Corporate stories will each have a robust social effect that brings humans together bodily and psychologically, and agency have an effect on via some of systems. Corporate memories need to faucet into customized elements that permit the speaker (narrator) to create a context in sync with the thoughts and aspirations of the receivers themselves, making the narrative greater charming in the workplace. Corporate storytelling can offer an possibility variable of knowledge and connection which cannot be done in isolation thru facts and facts. Storytelling is, consequently, an natural, attractive and deeper method of communiqué at some stage in a numerous target audience in an company, as memories inspire listeners to attract their private private elements and are available to the identical stop because the storyteller's predetermined quit.

Corporate testimonies also can want to empower employees and generate a memorable message that permits employees to take the lead and movement in tune with the standards of the business enterprise. The intention and goal of the usage of employer storytelling are greater relevant than just enjoyment and require consequences related to improving or improving conduct, necessities, and evaluations.

Corporate testimonies have historically been correlated with the emphasis on safety, well-being and lowering risk. Internal PR significance no matter the reality this is residing inside the storytelling of organizations as a manner to persuade, empower and encourage personnel in the direction of their employer, brand, and techniques. Several companies switch to storytelling as a way to extra correctly have an impact on their human capital. The query is raised: How to craft a decent business enterprise story?

There are three ranges to bring together a incredible corporate story.

1. BRING A PEN AND PAPER AND START WRITING ABOUT YOUR PAST, PRESENT, AND FUTURE:

Your company and brand story continues with the founder, and why she or he in truth started out the organization first. Don't spare every one of a kind detail, and compose that tale as a ancient and actual source from the begin. Involve anecdotes, fun facts and a sworn statement of what the agency has carried to this degree. Every strong logo tale takes the objective and dream of the economic business enterprise employer's beginning into interest, and spotting what has introduced you to this degree and in which the enterprise is heading is a stable location to begin. Label out the additives that show your organization's time table.

2. SUMMARIZE THE EXISTENCE OF YOUR COMPANY

Your commentary approximately your brand is a few element you're going to mention externally, so that you need to be revolutionary and also have a laugh with it. It is neither a middle project nor a imaginative and prescient announcement; a brand declaration takes into consideration what makes a distinction to customers and stakeholders and the agency's broader purpose. It extends past the cash you want to advantage and devices, driven in ideas, a virtually best future to gather for. It questions, "What are we doing proper here?" and "How are we going to make the area a better spot?" In answering the ones questions, you may discover the muse via which the announcement may be centered.

3. CRAFT THE STORY AROUND THAT STATEMENT:

The argument you generated in step becomes the baseline for what will become your emblem tale and you are planning to put in writing a one-internet internet page document to lower returned it up. A awesome tale about the emblem is concise and well-known the logo's records, such as in which you initiated from and in that you're heading. A excellent tale approximately the logo must be real, true and sincere. This won't be made up or extracted; customers in a 2nd element out the inauthenticity and blame you for it. There should moreover be a robust logo plot deeply rooted in motive if the story is stimulated by using manner of the usage of a reason the readers connect and interact with. This encourages the listener to be part of in that you are headed and is extemporaneously written. It famous your spirit and why you are doing what you're doing, and as a story, you want to discover ways to apprehend it in a masterly way.

Every brand calls for commercial organization activation. We need to discover how and while to tell our tale, in which to reveal it and the way to use it as a creativity release platform. Secondly, make sure your brand is hooked up collectively together with your narrative. To enhance your brand within the course of the story, compare your content material cloth, the logo fairness and assets you have got and your brand touch-elements. A strong emblem story need to additionally inspire mind for campaigns that correspond together with your purpose and help deliver a normal message to generate leads throughout the marketing rollouts.

Chapter 10: Crafting Of Captive Business Employer Narrative

1. Captivity narratives and the motive

Narratives of captivity are anecdotes of individuals recorded from uncivilized international locations thru warring parties. In the ones narratives, there may be a motif of redemption through notion. The captivity narrative medium is a long way too huge. Moreover, the importance of captivity and narrativization at stake within the development of the medium globally is simply really worth remembering: captivities in their heaps, producing narratives in their loads. Figures just like the ones assist the center, prototypical relevance of the fashion, mainly inside the American lifestyle, at the same time as they suggest the impossibility of stepping on a fixed definition of it or of the cultural artwork is practiced. No doubt the worldview of captivity changed through the years. Captivity narratives are a common storyline, plot or narrative. Stories of attack, trauma, recovery, and survival appear to healthy the ever-well-known romantic trope and appeal to primitive human emotions. As the fashion grew well-known, everyday scenarios have become greater repetitive, and the practical approach have become greater innovative. The Captivity Narrative little by little have end up a famous plot tool in American film and literature.

THE CRAFTING STRATEGY:

The crafting method of the captive employer narrative has five ranges.

STAGE1: THE ULTIMATE COMPANY STORY

It should include examples of the organization's iconic programs and strategic tasks, a evaluation of the business enterprise lifestyle and style, in addition to the capability units required. How would possibly you finish this story, as a captive owner or manager? Do you have got thoughts and programs that distinguish your captive from genuinely every person else to be had who might be vying for the identical talents pool? Have you indulged your panel in debates across the tale so that they might abruptly narrate in the occasion that they've been to satisfy a functionality system candidate somewhere? If now not, what's going to preserve you from crafting the narrative?

STAGE2: GLANCE AT THE MAGIC

This way making sure that the mere concept gets your employer and/or dept to peer in movement. It implies more than inviting him or her to a convention room and appearing an interview. To get a right revel in of the industrial organization, the chance have a good way to interacting with the opposite human beings concerned.

Know what kind of image may want to a capability recruit get as a captive owner or manager from travelling your place of work and getting near-up perspectives of the operations? Would he or she walk away with amazement or confusion? If the latter is much more likely, how will you alter the have an effect on you're looking to make?

STAGE3: CREATE AN APPROACH LIKE A LASER

Continuously optimize the quest emphasis and ensure you get to the satisfactory people. This isn't a modern-day or very modern idea. Moreover, captives want to understand that it is difficult to discover even minimally licensed applicants, given the unemployment price. The recruitment strive requires ordinary hobby to recruiting and keeping the crop's cream.

STAGE4: USING INVESTIGATIVE SKILLS

Hidden talents aren't positioned without issue. Do not even turn out to be settling for online activity advertisements and device forums. Use all available belongings and spend the preferred time to do the procedure effectively. Make fine you nicely hire the selection team, staff, captive managers and distinct expert gear. The wider you are making an strive, the more likely you may discover the hidden gem. With every person searching at team of workers, on the way to be triumphant you need to skip beyond and beyond your competing companies. Note, the alternative fees a horrible task match may be a lousy lot more costly than the cash spent earlier for an extensive are attempting to find.

STAGE5: THE POSTMORTEM:

Only after the quest has been completed effectively generates a complete analysis of what labored and what desires converting. Also, accumulate a list of the alternative finalists so that you have a baseline for any new positions a very good manner to open in the coming years.

A short test for captives is in case you were requested to provide a listing of 5 licensed applicants for your company for key positions, should you? Recruitment is an ongoing method. Generate a listing of human beings you meet who, for a few purpose, initiate you. That list becomes the thing of reference for functionality new employees.

Although the extent of unemployment may additionally additionally furthermore rise inch because the marketplace continues to relax, the conflict is relentless for pinnacle skills. Business Captives want to renowned this truth and make certain that they're constantly in recruitment mode, even though there are not any spots to be had.

2. Why are the Captivity narratives so well-known?

The implication that the narratives of captivity say a totally unique story about the interrogation of racial and gender standards is not completely awesome from a simplistic rationalization that the tales had been distinguished and famous because of the a laugh they supply to view the area from some different way. Expanding the captivity narratives to a super prospect is what many readers discover so attractive.

Business research

The twin prism of storytelling and sense-making

This is a fairly complex global. We cannot ensure something, and new demanding situations, sports, and shocks that shake our brains are constantly coming close to us. How are we to make logical sense of a few aspects that we discover so overseas? Well, the concept of creating senses lets in us to make experience of such complexities. This trouble count number offers with how people mirror, apprehend and test the frameworks they devise in response to their environment/activities and how the ones positive models are performed.

Human beings are because of this-making machines and are pretty nicely at crafting and producing recollections to provide an cause for the state of affairs whilst challenged with complexities and headaches. Sense making is herbal variability in human beings that, coupled with in advance information, offers which means that to enjoy, primarily based on new inputs. Sense making is predominantly an character act, notwithstanding the reality that we can also additionally moreover do it in groups and businesses. It permits clear up demanding situations in the articulation, trouble structuring, analysis generation, and adductive thinking. This hassle don't forget indicates at the place of growing the revel in-making and growth time table in dynamic organization fields which is probably marked through way of radical innovation and it suggests that both revel in-making and intention building are important cognitive mechanisms at some degree in the place of job surroundings.

Sense making in employer sectors narrates in career-statistics interviews with organization leaders. It uncovers how legitimately their reports and views of putting in vicinity their profession possibilities internal and beyond large companies make revel in. In this gift generation wherein reputations are tough-obtained however effortlessly out of vicinity, business business enterprise pioneers need to hold a actual story that is socially attractive if their careers are to live at the right music.

This can also well represent them inside the modern-day development of their enterprise business enterprise journeys. The cycle of sense making is a gadget of getting to know and reminiscences will be inclined to be the mechanistic clarification of sense making.

Sense making is a time period that applies to answer to the sector and sports sports spherical us, particularly new and uncommon stimuli, getting the aspect of, and responding upon them. The concept of sense making is essential for enterprise employer groups if you need to useful resource the personnel to live beforehand of the game or react to sports for which no suggestions or guidelines were advanced.

Sense making can be used to do the whole thing, from sculpting future consumer behavior to reacting to an unanticipated crisis in which no rules have been constructed. For instance, you'll be challenged with finding out in which way a line of merchandise want to be extended. The possible factors worried, which incorporates which route to get it in, which items to supply, who the customers can be, how the customers will reply, what the outcomes might be, and so forth, will want to make feel. This will all require a couple of sense making houses. Business stories 3 degrees wherein feel-making is an important element.

STAGE1: THE SOCIOCULTURAL CONTEXT

It applies, among one-of-a-kind factors, to the truth that the formation of senses is a social interest, and that it could make experience of something via a giving and taking mechanism among or more people in a place of job.

STAGE2: PERSONA IDENTIFICATION

The making of senses is contingent at the feel maker. One man or woman may additionally have a couple of meanings of an event than a few exceptional feel makers, with the identical case.

STAGE3: RETROSPECTION AND CONTEMPLATION

Peoples make sense of things via contemplating the state of affairs and the happenings.

Business interactions in sense making and storytelling correspond to mechanisms thru using which ' humans produce what they apprehend ' the term ' equivocality elimination ' is beneficial as it without problem is conscious that each exploration and innovation are additives of sense making. The belief of equivocality drives humans to gain and understand out of doors indicators and to apply them to ' make revel in ' of sports and put into impact their environments. Therefore, sense making requires not really perception and development of which means that however the tremendous authoring of conditions in which reflexive people are concerned and try to apprehend. People interact in partially contradictory cycles in which they devise ' realities ' after which make enjoy of them retrospectively in an ongoing cycle of experimentation and creativeness wherein personalities and social systems are each interpreted and invented. Sense making and commercial enterprise business organizations contain every different ' which has end up so essential and so embedded in our perceptions, theories and organizational research.

In phrases of ' software application ' sense making has regularly been especially interested in character and collective choice-making and network and commercial enterprise enterprise improvement mechanisms. Examine how choice choice-making takes region with the beneficial useful resource of ' realistic deliberation ' mechanisms based on discursive systems (candidate versions and recruitment picks) which can be themselves the made from committee-sense making. Selectors, they negotiate, artwork with a retrospective-ability mind-set to align variations and selections discursively-on the identical time as at the same time constructing. People inside and outside corporations are increasingly more confronted with new conditions which may be imbued with dynamic complexity. Making revel in with the aid of way of way of planning techniques, and looking for a logical approach to the question "what is the tale? It requires a fusion of sufficient sophistication of idea. This encapsulates the belief that on the same time as sensing is a balancing act among questioning and performing in a modern day global that owes much less to the tales and frames of the day past, maintaining up with the times modifications the equilibrium factor for rationalization thru movement. This empowers us to get the idea of sense making greater certainly.

Chapter 11: How To Shake Up Your Storytelling Fashion

Storytelling characterizes the tale-sharing social and cultural hobby, from time to time with virtuosity, theatrics, or adornment. Each culture has its private stories or narratives which might be communicated as a way to excite, teach, maintain life-style or sell moral ideas. If you are in search of to experience a tremendous storytelling fashion, right right here are eleven innovative strategies to attempt:

1. THE PASSIONATE YOU:

What is it that fascinates you? What do you dream approximately? What did you experience doing while you have got been young? Tackle with have a observe and observations and creativity. You'll find out stories across the manner and your satisfaction will come through your expressions in sharing positive testimonies. Pursue your ardour.

2. EXPOSE THE HIDDEN PERSON IN YOU:

Statements and dates are fantastic for constructing curriculum vitae, but stories are the outstanding method to reveal, no longer telling. By composing about key moments, whether or no longer the ones times are existence-changing tales or very not unusual occurrences, percentage your story (or your fundamental man or woman story).

3. EXPERIMENT:

No want to write down reminiscences with a keyboard. Try other storytelling factors — quill and paper, audio recording, picture, drawing, sketching, prancing, and guitar solo. Another method is probably better organized for your tale than others. Or you will be portraying numerous aspects of the equal storyline via gambling with a couple of favor.

4. SURROUND YOURSELF WITH CERTAIN LIMITS:

If you have were given a time restrict or your fashion of terms is restrained, you push yourself to compose the maximum critical pieces. Perceive a TV business corporation; it could take 15 or 30 or 60 seconds, but it wants to genuinely and concisely communicate statistics and feelings. Which story packs the most hit? What is it you have to strip out?

5. SLOW DOWN AND RELAX:

Pay interest after which see. Keep your eyes and ears loose and, inside the maximum unexpected locations, you can discover tales. Write them down, with consistent self-discipline. Pick every word cautiously. Read and re-observe the terms until you're certain you've got counseled the tale exactly what it want to be.

6. EXPLORE YOURSELF AND LIVE YOUR STORIES:

Learn new things; excursion; speak with human beings. Defy yourself Enjoy an interesting and charming tale so you need to broadcast it. Write down your impressions and others have a threat to live with you.

7. HAVE A DEFENDER AND A DEMON:

Stories want to have a defender and a crook mastermind-a hero and an enemy are frequently termed. The enemy might be a few thing inside the hero, like a barren region or "the system" or possibly paranoia. The plotline is how the hero overcomes the enemy. Things to impeach you about this could include: What're my purchasers or colleagues ' vital enemy? Is it difficult? Squandered coins?

8. THE USE OF CONTROVERSY AND CONFLICT:

Conflict and controversy are the manifestations of friction round enemy and hero. Perhaps it turns up as soon as the hero intends to skip the barren place, or perhaps whilst, the employer owner, decide to begin figuring out how to conquer a brilliant trouble. Clash additionally explains the stressful conditions you've got got faced on your avenue to achievement, whether or not or no longer they were banking issues or catastrophe troubles. If the individual does now not have a conflict then it's a pointless story.

9. OMISSION OF ANY INSIGNIFICANT THING:

Omit any specifics that do not pressure the plot upwards or the characters increase. It's about keeping the focus at the readers. Do no longer inform them about the motorbike in the event that they do now not need to listen about your purple motorcycle to apprehend the collection of your story. Do not inform them about the strolling shoes within the occasion that they don't need to pay interest what kind of awesome, excessive-tech shoes you used to stroll down the barren location.

10. THE TONE:

This is a reasonably smooth one. Stories with Formal-speaking ruins. Talk as you typically do. Appoint a storyteller, in case you seem a touch too formal to qualify as an average individual.

11. DONT FORGETS TO ADD SURPRISE:

A story is awful, without a surprise. You normally understand that however it desires to be repeated. Whether it's far a satisfied marvel or a horrific surprise, there can be as a minimum one surprise to each terrific tale. That is crucial to a contradictory story.

WHERE SHOULD YOU APPLY SUCH TECHNIQUES?

THE BLOG:

You can also additionally need to use your blog to offer an reason behind the entire model of your narrative in a fragmented way or you could use each weblog article as a micro-story. That tells an advanced phase of your narrative. Or you would probably create a weblog placed up approximately clients who emerge as managing something and the manner they tackled it as you launch a weblog put up with the micro-tale.

THE USE OF VISUAL MEDIA:

By building a video or animating it, any tale you can consider about yourself or your employer or your enterprise region or your customers can be made better.

INSPIRING EMPLOYEES:

Stories are a great device whether or not you are attracting new personnel or inspiring modern-day ones. The recollections are a way of explaining the cosmos. How would probable you describe the ancient beyond in a tale about your organization?

Another method to shake up your fashion inside the route of storytelling is to construct "TENSION IN A SCENE". A exquisite tale is constructed round tension. The unfortunate issue is that each day we come across anxiety in our very personal lives. The incredible news is, the aid for our narratives is tremendous. So, how do you assemble tension on your episodes to create that enjoy in your audiences?

Tension is caused as quickly as some factor is closely stretched, and even as combatants pull in commands at the equal time. We must use three additives to create tension in our scenes.

CONFLICTING GOALS:

Think of a previously seemed e-book or movie, and take a look at whether you can't appear to find out personalities with opposing desires. They are almost commonly visible: the parents who virtually want one life for their daughter at the same time as pursuing every different, the detective who strives to get to the lowest of the mystery an assassin is trying to conceal or the person who fell in love alongside along together with his excellent mate even as she is pursuing each different. Conflicting dreams and desires.

A RAISE IN STAKES:

This may go without mentioning, however if the personalities do now not care approximately the opposing desires, then the stress is destroyed. Raise stakes to decorate uncertainty and confusion. The stakes should be some issue that the character really cares approximately. The dilemma is to help the reader in spotting why the ones stakes matter quantity plenty.

TIME MANIPULATION:

Finally, time management will heighten tension. Occasionally tension is due to having the characters race in competition to the clock on a cut-off date, like a cruise missile ticking down. Over time managing functionality fanatics at threat reasons anxiety. Note the feature period can play in elevating the anxiety and placed it to use to construct pleasure or struggle.

The Ideas to take over the art

As for social media, permits admit it; the entirety is quite clean to do. We were all on pinnacle of factors. Whether it's miles taking walks a weblog, sharing a picture on Instagram sharing the current-day updates on Twitter or LinkedIn symptoms, are we doing so deliberately, or are we just performing some factor, most effective filling the streams of the social structures in our employer?

For any company or organization that uses social media to reveal exquisite reminiscences or their product line, and communicate with their clients or representatives, this is virtually a relevant query for them. But it could also belong to an entity if they may be inclined to correctly frame their ' expert and successful self ' in the international marketplace. It may have a huge effect on how people view what we placed up on our social networks and in the end engage with our brand. Stories may be ' micro, ' however it is able to be ' massive and big ' in combination. That's why we want to contemplate the memories we generate more carefully and dynamically, now not in isolation however as a much broader body of hard work. Though you could constantly construct effect with a chunk of content, that is maximum in all likelihood an exception to the ruling. But if you could continuously run reminiscences that thread with each exclusive and enlarge on the media-going via narrative of your business enterprise over the years, you will be uniquely positioned not best to draw site visitors but also to encourage and impact people in some manner. The thoughts to take over the art of effective storytelling are:

1. THE DIFFICULTY TO BEGIN:

Everybody is procrastinating, however while script commences, the way to tell whether or not you are a storyteller is to check your conduct. How regularly do you get into the waft on the same time as writing? Are the mind and thoughts disintegrating? Do you find the clock runs out and needs you had started tons earlier? Do you turn out to be trying extra vocabulary than you (or your target marketplace, crucially) will? You are a storyteller, Oh yea!

To trick, push or coerce yourself into getting off the floor, do some issue you want to do.

2. THE DISCIPLINE:

It's fun being a hit man, innit? Giggling on goals and on foot from responsibility? Not honestly. All which means which you may no longer be telling your story. And you're not going to be paid. In that feel, the arena we live in is not your buddy. We disappear inside the diversion. Discipline wishes to be enforced on a big massive variety of humans: transfer off the Wi-Fi; depart the Smartphone on mute and in a cupboard; sit down some other vicinity; supply large headphones; get the actual art work finished first; reward yourself later on.

3. KEEP LEARNING THE RULES:

There is lifelong learning to be determined in reminiscences, and there may be some different bunch of getting to know a way to formulate them. Technology, Tools, and Trapping. Very few shortcuts are to be had and none in reality worth considering.

4. CREATIVITY IS EVERYTHING:

It is even more vital, in a advertising and marketing and marketing framework, that your consumer is effortlessly centered. They'll excellent experience the content cloth even as they are comfortable with the layout, and that is wherein your creativity is available in. The precise take, the superb twist, the amazing moment. All readers are hoping for are those rewards. When they want a mystery they'll be going to get a Sudoku.

5.   THE ONLY IMPORTANT THING IS MAINTAINING THE AUDIENCE:

You want to be understood, as a skilled storyteller. It's the Town's only choice. Don't be socially awkward about it (the customers will in truth no longer be paying you to percent their memories). So because of this that you will examine your non-public writing to an outdoor attitude, even while you are writing:

Is this thrilling?

Is that a glowing sentence turn?

Would you need to analyze more?

Why are you going to tell me we are residing in a brief-paced, ever-changing worldwide, time and again?

Discover and include what has a tendency to artwork (and why) as an detail of your storytelling method. Whether you are writing a story as a ardour mission or hitting the organization deadlines Monday morning does no longer depend – analyzing the manner you determine as a storyteller is almost as important as understanding how the tale works. Recognizing your targets, your ' communiqué spheres ' and material troubles, oh and of path the sort of impact you are attempting to carry out, wants to be factored into.

Chapter 12: The Real Struggle

The model of storytelling on an organizational degree

Storytelling is a treasured device that invokes visible images and sentiments which is probably more. It has a huge effect on corporation owners who can tell a powerful tale. This gives a paradigm and examples of enterprise storytelling, explores using memories in managerial growth, and highlighted strategies to enhance storytelling skills for managers and executives. One aim of managerial boom is to seize the creativeness and hobby of the man or woman and offer the motivation for non-prevent development. Stories can be used to illustrate in fact every key detail of an organization. Stories can be regarding customer service, incentives, idea, manner of lifestyles expectations, stereotyping, control, management, manage, manage, coordination, selection-making, art work (dis)satisfaction, and so on. Stories can be simplistic and unique, or complicated.

Stories make it easier to maintain in thoughts the facts, and greater practicable. We are a effective method of changing beliefs, mind, and expectancies. Stories are generally extra green than information and facts. Every listener perceives him/her in a story and compares it subconsciously to his / her non-public enjoy, asking questions like "If did anything like this display up to me?"

We take into account what befell to us, so our private experience is more unforgettable than an occasion that took place to 3 other human. Stories represent a sizable kind of features: they inspire, invoke emotion, spark seen memories, and support hold in thoughts of the illustrated statements on top of things development. A tale being informed aloud has triggered better information of phrases and ideas relative to the identical story provided as TV software. The TV version produced superior outcomes most effective even as specific story acts have been remembered. Stories counseled of excessive conceptual imagery phrases induced better lengthy-time period records retention than repetition, or rotating and drilling.

The most effective memories are honest, exceptional imagery and sensible communicate, with some repetitive components of the story In order to undertake storytelling on an organizational degree, one want to maintain a few key factor in mind.

1. The organizational memories ought to be structurally sound and tell approximately real people, give an reason at the back of actual sports activities and actions, be set in a time and place that the purpose market can renowned and perceive with, and must be associated with the ideology and/or way of lifestyles of the organization.

2. The recollections additionally need to be not unusual organizational or unit records. Not only do humans want to understand the tale to attain fulfillment in expressing lifestyle, but similarly they need to apprehend that others comprehend it, and obey its help.

3. The effective story about the organization explains a social settlement, whether or not topics are completed in the agency or not. Stories encourage the reader to recollect organization policies, incentives, and effects without the exercising of trial and blunders.

Moreover, in an tremendous story the five logical elements, or steps, are:

Setting:

Moment, spot, the context. A storyteller captures the essence or state of affairs in which the audience can step into at the identical time as portraying the placing on an organizational stage.

Construct-up ("predicted problem!"):

A chain of sports warning listeners that "the hassle is growing!"

Disaster or climax:

It's the excessive point or quit of the story. This is the big occasion important as masses because the storyline-something takes area!

It can be expected, however if the story takes a jump or turn, it often comes as a surprise. A new element is periodically inserted into the sport.

Practicing:

What that applicable character has decided. We infer or right now specific in this a part of the narrative what the hero/heroine found out from the financial disaster.

New conduct or attention:

This demonstrates the unique actions and/or information of the primary character because of the motion, the morality of the tale. The focal issue in this very last step is preserved knowledge. Get to discover ways to lock the touch circle. Suppose you do now not get it. The target market did no longer continually pay interest what the speaker intended.

The three discourses

The "Story" pertains to the actual chronology of occasions in a tale; "Discourse" relates to a certain tale being manipulated in the narrative presentation. Therefore these terms communicate with the essential shape of all types of the narrative.

a. The Premodern discourse:

Premodern discourse combines zeal and philosophical mirrored image with preindustrial felony recommendations and customs, and even patriarchal ones. It does now not distinguish an character from his / her societal or non secular characteristic: associate, soldier, and masses of others. The premodern debate is a mystical and nomadic quest that permits handwork, manner of existence, network, and a deep enjoy of community over rationality inside the economic device.

b. The postmodern discourse

The very first method to postmodern shape is primarily based completely at the idea of a previous era's displacement. This method, but, can be brushed off as a non-discursive and materialist worldview. Postmodern discourse de-facilities the man or woman entity and protects living and collective beings in opposition to the gripping storyline, artificial, and sensible order of factors.

c. The modernist discourse

The modernist discourse aimed toward taming premodern pagan and mythological ardors, containing the feudal bribery of absolute monarchy. Modernist existence stories represent the extensive society that is dominated, rationally prepared, which harnesses premodern emotion, subjectivity, and desire.

Homan gadgets to the perception that transformation takes area first-rate even as it is handled. Change takes vicinity in agencies all of the time. And the humans-to-human beings interactions in corporations are an massive motor for that exchange. The reminiscences they tell each special and people they increase and put into effect collectively assist in shaping the "mini-worlds" inside the corporation to which Homan refers. These worlds have their own command, related to percentage reminiscences, shared reviews and shared obvious fact approximately what is heading on and what had to be carried out approximately it that ties these mini-worlds round each awesome. Adaptation of storytelling inside the business enterprise zone is in a unmarried way a sensible example of story hierarchical shape inside an company. It's additionally an goal to paintings closer to in wonderful approaches. The last purpose may be this model's self-conscious version, adjusting itself constantly to be greater efficient.

Corporate recollections, co-created memories, and man or woman stories are all simultaneously positioned inside the company.

The organization tales encompass the signposts, the feel of course, the values of the corporation, the approach that is conveyed pinnacle-all the way all the way down to control, and all of the employees who paintings beneath it. However co-created testimonies encompass the feel, facts, misconceptions and perceptions that people percent. We may be fairly considered one in every of a type inside an corporation most of the a couple of departments and cliques. They're furthermore seen in the vintage hierarchy as reacting to the organization story. In an organizational shape, private reminiscences may additionally appear very beside the factor. They can be stereotyped as inane matters shared across the coffee maker and counseled within the comfort of domestic and family among many close to co-human beings or suggested others approximately the task. There may be very little credence inside the potential of personal narratives to regulate the vintage system's company memories. Unless it appears to be of course the CEO's unique or personal tale... So they name it VISION.

How to end up a Master Storyteller - The Secret Sauce

Many people seem to remember that reading the art work of effective storytelling is a complex and tough piece of the puzzle, unique simplest for top notch professional people of society. This could not be any further from truth. The skills required to tell a powerful tale can be determined out thru education and training, and honestly everyone can turn out to be a draw close storyteller with the right toolkit. Whether you're hoping to draw new clients or fun the triumphing ones, the direction to move is the great storytelling. It stretches past terms, which involve pix and movies-the idea stays the same. During your trips and activities, the clients will percentage their opinions and recollections approximately their interactions. And, clearly as you are a part of developing the tour revel in, you have to additionally be the only to inform the story. You want to realize the art of effective storytelling; right right right here is how.

AUDIENCE ANALYSIS:

This preliminary step is critical and could have a look at the duration of the narrative and which vocabulary you ought to use. Until you begin your tale make investments 5 mins in considering who you want to goal.

To whom are you referring? Boomers or Millennials? Were they attempting to find expensive or price-pleasant critiques? Need to step all through a greater severe tone or is a polite sound going to artwork smarter? Will or not it's shared as a weblog article, on Twitter, or on a brilliant platform? These are very precious elements to maintain in mind in assisting you place the right mood and with the audience to make sure favorable consequences.

MAKE THEM CARE AND STAY FOCUSED:

You want to sense on your visitors whether or no longer or not socially, culturally or aesthetically and cause them to care. In our manner of lifestyles, in which people usually will be predisposed to brush over topics and scroll over content that is big. Why ought to the tale reason them to taking an interest? What does it depend to the goal marketplace? Clarify on your head at the same time as building the tale, because of the truth if it's far no longer obvious to you, the audience might not comprehend it.

Tip: Start writing it on a post-it, and positioned it for your counter to reassure you why this story desires to be counseled.

PLOTTING THE SCENE:

We have interaction with the arena via the use of our sensations and so if you assume your goal market to be absolutely captured, you need to prompt their sensations. Set the scene, and provide an cause of the story for your audience.

Where did the tale cross? How did the environment heady scent? Has this felt like pine needles on the lowest of a wooded region? Or similar to the beach? Where ends the journey? By getting worried to your goal marketplace's sensations and setting the tone, you can carry your audiences a greater interactive enjoy.

THE CREATIVE CHRONOLOGY:

Sometimes you'll likely choose out to plunge the reader proper into the center of all of the drama or to maintain their reputation until the cease of the tale. This is likewise one of the great techniques for your tale to stimulate pride, anticipation, and strain. When the goal market does no longer recognize what is taking location, they will maintain on reading to locate the sport's missing bits. Consider the reality, though that audiences do not want to work out Sherlock Holmes on their cell phone so do not make this new Rubik's Cube your tale.

THE PUNCHLINE:

What is the goal of storytelling? Do not forget about that regardless of the truth which you try this to probably sell products or services, the client shouldn't experience that manner. The tale may be humorous, profitable, sentimental, or a mishmash of those, or something else altogether. Be progressive but do now not hesitate to constantly make it extra exciting and critical.

THE RESOLUTION, THE GRAND FINALE:

Even if the story maintains, and you intentionally carry together up the suspense, the tale needs to be closed. Whatever story you have created need to be efficiently finished and no queries want to be dropped dangling. Add a touch of magic to your tale via enforcing a sense of delight on your target market, the shape of emotion you get after a notable movie even as you go out the theater. You can try this with the useful resource of coming near them as they head to their accommodations with a "key query" approximately society or a few element much like fear about.

AVOID LIMITATION OF WORDS:

Even greater a photograph well really worth a thousand sentences and video clips. They will help your reminiscences written. This additionally indicates you may generate new phrases, supplied they will be impactful and the reader can be very well elaborated approximately their fee. Not simplest you thrill and amuse your fanatics via this, but you may moreover build your logo the use of cleverly invented terms and terms, moreover reworking them into one of a type hash tags to market it your enterprise.

ENJOYMENT, THE FINAL PROCESS:

You should additionally love reviving the sensation in your narratives as a first-rate deal as you loved growing the instantaneous. Think approximately it logically: Anyone who reads it can keep on the journey you offer an entire life and can revel in it vicariously.

The Resolution

The role of the storyteller is challenging and whole of risks and moral implications. However while the economic business enterprise corporation's storytellers behave like rational thinkers, adventurers, and researchers they might get to the lowest of the seeds for improvement and growth in every the incorrect and the extremely good initiatives. Storytellers in the business organization have the functionality to help the tremendous memories propagate and evolve and come to be more and more real, more consistent with the ideals and undertaking of its employees and increasingly more inside the interest of creating an sincere determination to its customers and to the network as a whole. If we can do that, then we've have been given a powerful assistant for outstanding trade in the place of job and in our lives.

Chapter 13: Create Rapport With Them

Have you ever met everybody who had a completely unique manner of connecting to others? It didn't rely who they might meet. They managed to create information and take delivery of as proper with in just a few moments.

It virtually doesn't matter quantity what shape of company you are in or the placement you keep inside that industrial agency; you need to recognize strategies to build rapport so that you may have all forms of opportunities. Once you have have been given created rapport with others, they will do their excellent to help you attain success.

There are those who will argue that that is something that may't be found out. It is some component that people are born with. You both have the capability to construct rapport, or you in truth can't. This isn't genuine. Rapport may be superior. If you've got were given already were given the functionality to construct rapport, you can enhance and nurture this capability similar to each different expertise.

If you don't recognize what rapport is, keep reading to find out what it is and strategies you can boom it.

Rapport is a dating or connections you have got were given with some different individual. It is probably interpreted as a harmonious expertise among one man or woman or many humans. Rapport creates a relationship base this is harmonious, close, and meaningful among or greater humans. It is a connection you get as soon as you have met any individual which you accept as authentic with, like, and characteristic a perspective that you right away apprehend. It is a bond at the manner to form whilst you locate which you percentage the identical priorities and values in existence. Building rapport is a way that develops that connection.

There is probably times at the identical time because it virtually takes place without any strive on your component. Most people have had an revel in in which they've got truly "get on well" with each other person with out attempting. This is generally how youth friendships start. But you could growth and construct rapport consciously with the aid of manner of using being empathic and locating some not unusual ground.

This is basically pronouncing that rapport is an emotional connection to others. Building rapport is gaining knowledge of how to set up this connection. It is typically primarily based totally on perspectives or reports the people worried have shared, and this consists of a humorousness that is shared. Creating rapport seems to be maximum important at the start of a walking dating or meeting an acquaintance. This rapport would in all likelihood very last for plenty, some years.

If you've got got have been given a rapport with some distinct person, you'll percentage:

1. Coordination: you will revel in like you are "in sync" with each one-of-a-kind, and you percentage commonplace understandings.

Your body language, tone, and strength ranges can also be comparable.

2. Positivity: each of you're glad and fine, and you show scenario and take care of each particular.

3. Mutual attentiveness: each of you are interested in and targeted on what every different are doing or announcing.

This kind of connection may at once appear, or it'll slowly amplify with time. It could probably obviously develop, or you may make a factor to intentionally assemble it.

You don't just use rapport to assemble relationships; it could be your foundation to fulfillment in life. Once you have got have been given advanced a rapport with a person, you're inside the tremendous area to teach, look at, and characteristic an impact on, particularly whilst the do not forget you have got built manner others will receive your thoughts, they may be inclined to make new opportunities, and share facts with you.

It doesn't depend if you are enhancing a relationship, promoting topics, or going for a interest interview; know-how techniques you could collect rapport will help you do better.

Why Rapport Is Important

You need to have a rapport in each your private and professional lives. An company may also lease any person that they anticipate is going to paintings properly with the personnel they already have. Relationships which may be non-public are usually much less complex to make bigger whilst there can be a near know-how and connection among all of the occasions worried.

Anytime you meet someone new, you begin trying to gather a rapport. It doesn't remember variety whether or now not you want it; that is the reason small talk exists. It is the way you try to discover subjects that you have in common with others with a purpose to bring together a shared bond. This is vital considering that everybody has a bent to need to be round unique individuals who are like us.

It is lots less difficult to create rapport with others who are which encompass you or who proportion some of the equal pastimes. You should have hundreds of things to talk to them approximately, along side having a few shared floor. This makes communicating and building relationships masses lots much less difficult. But you would possibly have positioned yourself questioning: "They are lovable; I'm tremendous, but we don't have something in not unusual."

If you determined that operating with a person is going to be difficult, and verbal exchange is going to be very hard because you don't have a shared body of reference. You are going to have to work hundreds more tough to create rapport at the same time as growing a relationship, but it is viable.

Building Rapport

Rapport must be a connection amongst or extra people. This way that it isn't some thing that you may make on my own. But you may help it increase via way of using doing the subsequent:

1. Appearance

You could possibly have heard that the influence you're making whilst you first meet someone way plenty, and that is especially true. Your look is going to help you connect with others higher while now not developing barriers. The notable rule to comply with is to dress a piece better than whomever you will meet. But, in case you arrive and also you word that you have overdressed, you could get dressed all the way down to higher in form a few aspect state of affairs you are in.

2. Breaking The Ice

For some human beings, starting a conversation with someone new may be very stressful. You is probably compelled, at the side of having awkward mannerisms and body language. Developing rapport on the start of the conversation with new people can also moreover make the final results very terrific. It doesn't depend how disturbing or disturbing you may in all likelihood experience; the number one element you need to do is lighten up and stay calm. When you can decrease the anxiety, speaking gets tons much less hard, and rapport starts offevolved offevolved to develop.

Anytime you meet a person for the number one time, there are a few matters you can do to lessen the anxiety. This can assist every events enjoy comfortable and talk higher:

a. Use topics which might be steady for small speak. Talk approximately a few evaluations you can have shared, the manner you got to wherein you are in recent times, the weather, and so forth. Stay away from speakme approximately yourself too much and in no way ask the man or woman any direct questions.

b. Listen to what they are announcing and try to find out a few shared occasions or reports. This gives you masses greater to speak approximately.

c. Try using humor. Laughing can create harmony. You can shaggy dog tale about the situations, situation, or your self however by no means, ever make a comedian tale about the opportunity character.

d. Be aware about your body language and any signals you is probably sending. Keep eye contact for at the least 60 percent of the time. Lean inside the course of the other character slightly and loosen up. This indicates them which you are carefully being attentive to them.

e. Show empathy. Show them that you may see their thing of view. Keep in mind that rapport is more about finding what you've got in common and "being on extraordinary human beings's wavelengths. Having empathy can collect this.

Be sure the others worried feel protected but now not like they're being interrogated. Just like you'll in all likelihood enjoy uneasy or annoying speaking and assembly a person new, they could experience the equal way. If you could cause them to experience extra comfortable, you will be able to have a better conversation.

three. Keep The Basics in Mind

Keep in mind applicable conversation's fundamentals:

a. Never outstay your welcome

b. Listen attentively and carefully

c. Maintain top posture at all times and hold your head up

d. Remember the man or woman's name that you are talking to

e. Relax

f. Smile

g. Always be culturally appropriate

These fundamentals create a foundation for super communications. It goes to be very hard to create rapport whilst no longer having every of them. They also are going to help you create empathy, recall, and feelings in others which you pay interest nicely to them.

four. Common Ground

Finding a few common floor ought that will help you create rapport. You can use some small speak to decide out some subjects which you percentage.

Many human beings like to speak approximately themselves. If you may show them which you are truly inquisitive about them, they will lighten up and "open up." You can use some questions which are open-ended to find out private information. You may additionally have lengthy past to the identical college, you'll probably percentage the equal pastimes, you may have grown up within the same small city, otherwise you both just like the same sports activities activities organization. Just sharing the frustration of navigating via early morning visitors ought to help you get a piece towards others.

You need to don't forget to be honest and right and stay some distance from overdoing things. Never try to make un an thrilling tale and give up attempting too tough to create rapport. This will make you seem too decided, but it would positioned a dent on your credibility.

Laughter is the exceptional tool at the identical time as constructing rapport, however you want to apply it carefully. Not anybody is ready to tell jokes, and what might also moreover appear suitable to you can reason a person else to get indignant. If you trust you studied it is possible that your remark can be taken wrong, don't say it.

5. Find Experiences You Both Share

Rapport can in no way be grown with out human beings interacting with every awesome. The top notch way to have interaction with others is by way of way of way of creating shared, new reminiscences. These shared stories might be genuinely attending some conferences collectively or complicated like cooperating together on new techniques. Collaborating to apprehend troubles, locate answers, and designing strategies have to assist supply you in the direction of others.

6. Have Empathy

Empathy is understanding others by manner of being able to see topics from their perspective and understanding the emotions that they'll be experiencing. In order to percent and understand their mind-set, you need to realise what makes them tick. As I in reality have already said, maximum human beings like to speak approximately themselves, their dislikes and likes, their need and desires, their successes and issues. This approach you need to ask those open-ended questions after which take a seat lower once more and allow them to talk.

You must actually pay hobby everything they're saying, so you are capable of respond with hobby and intelligence. It is critical as a way to be a incredible listener on the equal time as extraordinary-tuning your intelligence emotionally. You also can exercising perceptual positions. This is a manner that allows you to appearance subjects from every other individual's mindset.

7. Mirror Them

Research has confirmed that we love being spherical others that we expect are like ourselves. Matching and mirroring are some strategies that help us assemble rapport through making ourselves like them.

The way you can do that is deeper than just the belongings you say. What we're pronouncing to others debts for approximately seven percentage of what we speak approximately our mind-set and feelings. How our voice sound is a bigger percent at 38 percentage. Body language is right spherical fifty five percent. You may additionally skip over a trick if you don't think about the complete photo while speaking about human communication.

You can try the ones techniques to help you build a few rapport:

a. Watch their frame language, which encompass their expressions, posture, and gestures. If they relaxation their chin on their left hand, reflect them with the useful resource of doing it collectively together with your proper. If you want to suit them, use your left.

b. Use the identical temperament. If they are extroverted or introverted, exuberant or shy, you want to behave for this reason. If they may be reserved, then you definately want to be reserved, too, or you would in all likelihood hazard being seemed as invasive or brash.

c. Use language that is similar. If they use direct, easy phrases, you want to use the equal phrases. If they talk slowly and softly, then lower your tempo and amount.

Common experience and discretion are critical at the identical time as you are matching and mirroring. Never mimic their each gesture and word. If you try this, you may probable cause them offense. Above all, you need to be diffused and attempt your satisfactory to find out a trouble in that you simply start certainly synchronizing their conduct; this can preserve them from noticing what you're doing.

Matching and mirroring is probably a bit difficult to apprehend however hold in mind which you unconsciously fit and replicate what our coworkers, friends, and households do every day. If you actually need to exercising this technique, strive performing some function-gambling.

Building Rapport Nov-Verbally

Having that first verbal exchange can also need that will help you loosen up, however there is lots of rapport constructing that occurs without any phrases being spoken. This takes place via non-verbal conversation.

You can preserve and create rapport by using the use of sending the alternative person signals that encompass tone of voice, facial expressions, eye contact, frame movements, and the manner you function your body. The next time you notice people speakme, watch how they mimic every other and use non-verbal verbal exchange.

You can boom rapport instinctively. It is our innate safety to avoid battle that a number of us try to stay away from that preserve us from constructing rapport speedy.

It is particularly important to use the proper body language. You have if you need to read and recognize what someone's frame language is making an attempt to inform you. Although you can try to steer others via verbal verbal exchange, if there isn't a awesome healthful between the property you're announcing and your body language, whoever you are speaking to is going to agree with your frame language. Creating rapport starts offevolved offevolved with using the proper frame language. This manner you need to be open, relaxed, and inviting.

Other than matching body language and listening to the character you're speaking to, it could additionally assist if you can healthful their words. Clarifying and reflecting lower returned on what they have got said are a few best processes to use to reveal them which you are being attentive to them. It gives you the opportunity to use terms and words that they used to show you have got some commonplace floor and similarities.

How you operate your voice is also critical at the same time as developing rapport. If you are nerve-racking or fearful, you will probably begin talking faster. This may want to make you sound even greater confused. We have a propensity to trade our tempo, amount, pitch, and alternate our voice to make the matters we're announcing extra interesting. It can trade the manner we encounter to others. Try to lose your tone and speak softer and slower. This will will let you create rapport much less tough.

How to Rebuild Rapport

It is going to make an effort to reestablish rapport after it modified into lost. The first component you need to do is figure out why you out of location it. You have to stay humble and simply offer an motive of as in truth as feasible what occurred. If you need to make an apology, then do it.

The next detail you want to do is find out a manner to repair that broken consider. Put in some greater art work when you have to, and regularly else, hold your word. Genuine problem and transparency for extraordinary's dreams move an prolonged manner in rebuilding and reestablishing rapport and recollect.

You create rapport as soon as you've got have been given advanced an affinity, friendship, and mutual take into account with others. Creating rapport will be very beneficial to your career. It assist you to establish interpersonal relationships, and this can open masses of doorways for you.

You can use the ones steps to help assemble rapport:

1. When sitting, lean in the course of the individual. Don't bypass your legs; preserve your arms and palms open. This is known as open frame language, and it will let you make the alternative individual loosen up.

2. Keep eye contact approximately 60 percent of the time. Try not to steer them to experience uncomfortable.

3. While listening, make encouraging gestures and sounds. Nod frequently

four. Smile

five. Use their name as early as viable inside the conversation. This isn't definitely well mannered, however it suggests them which you remembered their name

6. Ask them some open questions even as you take into account that they're much much less complex and additional cushty to reply

7. Stay some distance from contentious topics at the same time as talking. Stick with tour preparations, remaining speaker, or the climate. Avoid speaking about politics in any respect charges.

eight. Use remarks to make clean, replicate, and summarize to reveal them that you were listening. This enables make any misunderstandings less difficult to restoration.

nine. Find not unusual hyperlinks and communicate approximately subjects that display the opportunity what they were talking about

10. Show empathy. Show them that you recognize how they enjoy, and you are able to see topics from their attitude.

eleven. If you receive as authentic with what they have got stated, inform them so and provide an reason in the back of why.

12. Build on their mind

13. Don't be judgmental inside the route of them. Release all stereotypes and any mind which you could have drawn inside the route of them.

14. If you don't agree with them, provide them the reason first and then tell them which you don't agree.

15. If you don't recognize an answer, admit it. If you are making a mistake, admit it. Being sincere will continually be the exceptional manner to construct receive as real with.

sixteen. Be genuine to your self via the usage of using verbal and visible behavior even as running collectively to maxlmize your verbal exchange.

17. Stay a ways from criticizing, offer them compliments, and mainly else, be polite.

Creating rapport is needed for each issue of life. If you don't have rapport, you aren't going to have any form of courting.

Having the capability to construct rapport is extremely beneficial in each your professional and personal life. By having it as each other potential, way you could construct your relationships quicker on the same time as enhancing your communications. Your work relationships gets better, and any non-public relationship gets stronger.

Chapter 14: The Right Attitude And Power

The role mind-set plays in communique is an crucial one. When people are speakme with every different, they are wearing a certain thoughts-set that may have an impact at the final results of the communique and their relationship. Simply placed, there are 3 essential varieties of mind-set.

1. Positive Attitude

People with a top notch mindset will will be inclined to examine the brighter trouble of things, and that they select to give interest to answers in vicinity of creating conflict. They have a propensity to be more cooperative and glad, and they look for prevalent boom and now not genuinely their very very very own growth.

People with a superb body of mind will be predisposed to look greater achievement as they realise the blessings of speaking successfully, and that they implement that in their paintings. They paintings tough, and that they communicate properly with their managers. They are constantly looking for an answer, and they're ok with taking dangers and experimenting with matters to locate the proper answer. They also take delivery of the changes that get up.

They moreover find out it clean to speak with others whilst they may be satisfied in choice to in a sad country. We moreover commonly tend to experience loose to percentage our emotions and mind with a person who speaks in a powerful way. A fine mind-set allows to open the doorways of verbal exchange and the effects to be higher than closed verbal exchange.

2. Negative Attitude

A horrible mind-set will motive lousy verbal exchange, and the very last results is in no way beneficial. When we talk in a poor manner about our employers or buddies, it will create a unfavorable surroundings. The consolation in those situations will disappear while terrible conversation takes area, specifically with co-personnel and the better-ups. Negative communique will grow to be hampering the art work and could create a horrific intellectual usa for those who art work there. People's professional and personal lifestyles will undergo, so that you can area pressure on various relationships.

People connect to folks that are outstanding and disconnect at the identical time as they are bad. Negative conversation frequently results in the grapevine and might turn out to be inflicting humans to get fired if it isn't always controlled in a few way. If a student has terrible emotions in the direction of a sure teacher and talks badly about it, it's going to become hampering their relationship with that trainer and bring about extra troubles.

Negative verbal exchange in no manner offers you with an answer. The best thing it does is drowns a person in greater troubles that they could't appear to get away from. If there may be someone you don't like, don't unfold fake statistics approximately them. Try to modify the state of affairs or search for a specific function at the same time as you discover yourself trapped in terrible feelings.

three. Neutral Attitude

When someone has a independent attitude, they will frequently take the center route, and that they acquired't take a characteristic in conversation. However, the ones people are much less complex to deal with than terrible humans. They stay diplomatic, which has a bent to paintings in their pick out. They don't take a stand at the same time as speaking, making them more difficult to are watching for.

four. No Communication

This isn't an thoughts-set, however it is a problem that is frequently because of a horrible thoughts-set. No communication will purpose miscommunication. It is higher to remain communicative in place of uncommunicative due to the fact that has a tendency to bring about awful communicate.

There are some of situations which could arise whilst we are able to't communicate or say what the problem is, so that you can bring about aggravation. Everybody has to realize their need for communication. Employees want to be in direct communique with their business enterprise, and that they want as a manner to percentage information approximately their art work with them. A lack of communication in a commercial employer setting will purpose horrible communicate and hinder the growth of the worker.

It additionally shouldn't be as much as definitely the employee to communicate. If the higher-usa of americadon't communicate down the chain of command, then employees aren't going to apprehend what to do. People can also use a loss of conversation to make you a sufferer by way of strolling in opposition to you due to the fact they recognize you don't have communication skills.

Even for your non-public existence, a lack of conversation will reason troubles. If you're disenchanted with your partner approximately something, you need to apprehend that you may talk to them approximately it. Otherwise, if you maintain it bottled up, it's going to purpose terrible emotions closer to and an eventual blow-up.

Good verbal exchange in families allows to growth familial bonds. A easy text can paintings wonders.

How Attitude Affects Conversation

Perception and mindset should have an effect on any form of communication in horrible and quality tactics. Upbeat, extremely good, and respectful attitudes enhance all forms of communication. In a commercial company placing, this will beautify income, productivity, and morale. However, horrible verbal exchange behavior wishes to be treated in advance than it impacts the organisation corporation lifestyle or reasons the organization to crumble altogether.

Employees with excessive viewpoints may additionally moreover moreover locate it hard to appearance the mind-set of others due to the reality they all have an thoughts-set that the opposite must be incorrect with out taking a 2nd to investigate the scenario. Similarly, while employees have a similar mind-set, they may forget about moments of miscommunication due to the truth they anticipate they may be continuously in settlement.

How does an established thoughts-set have an impact on conversation? If a person has a company attitude about a few element, they'll be much more likely to talk approximately it from a black-and-white mind-set. For instance, in case you are without a doubt in competition to elevating business enterprise taxes, then the most compelling argument for raising the taxes received't be part of up because you acquire right here into it with a pre-gift attitude. This ingrained way of thinking will impact your capacity to recognize a few component apart from what you determined. Having an open thoughts facilitates deliver a boost on your inner surroundings, and it'll open up new doors to increase.

Whenever you've got a preconceived belief approximately some difficulty, it affects your potential to speak on the topic. For instance, if your boss got here as lots as you with an idea for an ad marketing campaign and you accept as true with that advertisements don't paintings, your thoughts-set is going to effect the communication that need to take region a few of the of you. Even in case your boss does a amazing machine at setting up the speak about the ad to assist obtain the goal demographic, your attitude goes to cloud your judgment. That's why you could't be too quick to decide. You need to typically pay hobby out any cheap proposals and recall them.

Attitudes also can effect a person's capability to as it need to be and completely communicate with every other. For example, in case you hired a new individual as a profits clerk who has an extensive history in such a feature, you can assume that she may also need to jump in without a excellent deal education. Your mind-set motives you to count on topics about her talents, and additionally you turn out to be skimming over education on strategies and guidelines greater than you may have had she been inexperienced. When you incompletely communicate in this way, it is able to have an all-round terrible pertaining to her potential to do her interest, that could affect productivity and create distrust among her and her coworkers. All new personnel have to be handled the identical and given the same system to get adjusted to the businesses necessities.

If your mindset is overly tremendous, it can moreover reason vain verbal exchange. For instance, if there's a challenge manager who believes that remaining-minute art work doesn't purpose issues, they will now not respond to reminders from staffers that superb additives of a task are finished or that the last date is in danger of no longer being met. With their mindset, the tries of communication with them don't take a look at in. This is a contagious kind of mind-set and can with out problems unfold thru the place of work, inflicting some of issues.

When colleagues have conflicting views, it may be hard for them to discover a way to speak politely. Their attitudes can also need to guide them to avoid each precise and limit all forms of interactions. This can motive miscommunication thinking about that neither celebration wants to breakthrough and take duty. If an employment dispute isn't resolved indoors an much less pricey quantity of time, or it begins offevolved to create problems inside the place of work, it's time to intervene.

www.ingramcontent.com/pod-product-compliance
Lightning Source LLC
Chambersburg PA
CBHW070735020526
44118CB00035B/1356